MONEY MACHINES FOR LIFE

Maximize Your Human Life Value, Social Security Income, and Defined Benefit Pensions

Jim Lusk, CFP®, CLU®, ChFC®, CLF®, MEd

WITH
Nicholas McCaskey

Preface

I am writing this book in memory and honor of the late great, Marty Polhemus, General Agent of a top 5 mutual company for over 3 decades. Under his leadership the agency in "little" Spokane, Washington went from a small office, about 80th rank in production out of about 100 GAs to number 5 (number 1 West of the Mississippi) in the company. I was fortunate enough to be hired by Marty and train under him and his team of leaders for 6 months before he retired. His Second Line Manager, mentor and friend, Jim Bockemuehl, trained and developed me within the "Polhemus method" during those formative years (1-5) and I will be forever grateful. This great "winning culture" produced many mentors for me that have affected my whole career. Professionals like Ed VanVliet, Bob Bishopp, Kent Lupton, Dave Altmeyer, Kent Beebe, the late David Trail, Paul Hanson (current GA) and many more helped shape my career around values of quality service, integrity, honesty, and needs based financial counseling.

In 1995, I left that great company because I felt I had a better track to upper management and took a position as a direct appointment with another high- rated, mutual company in Eugene, Oregon. Thanks go to Steve Bakke, MP (Managing Partner) and Mike Keone, RVP (Regional Vice President), for taking a chance on me and letting me integrate my tried and tested methods into that already successful culture. In 9 years in Eugene, I worked with such great advisors as Dave Hakko, Ray Lemke, Rory Robison CFP, Amy O'Donnell and Lorraine Lyons. Rick Hayes MSFS, one of the best trainers and developers in the industry was also part of that successful culture.

I was fortunate in 2004 to be promoted to a first-line manager as the MP for the great state of Minnesota with over 100 advisors. There I got to work with more incredible professional advisors like Dr Lee Kitzenberg,

Dave Duchene, Terry Lewis, Dale Wawracz, David Simonson, Jim Johnson, Jeff Green, Sue Zweiner, Char Rigelman, Ron Meyer, and more. I had the pleasure of recruiting the great Tom Miller, CFP (current MP in Montana), Eric Herried, Ashish Tomar, Gordy Struss and many others. This was also a time I developed peer relationships with Industry greats who have mentored me more than they can imagine. I have to give credit to great MPs (or equivalent leaders) whom I had the privilege of associating with like: Mike Scovel, Tigran Basmadjyan, Peter McAvinnn, Bill Terry, Puneet Seth, Sal Farina, Kevin Choi, Mark Madgett, Mark Byron, Mark Kostovich, Steve Ray, Steve Braden and many more. What a great company of first class powerful leaders!

After 7 years of cold winters, I took an office opening in Fresno, California.

My incredible wife, Debbie (of 48 years June 2024) informed me that there was 330 days of sunshine there, so we should take it. Well, great choice, "happy wife, happy life". That was a wonderful 5 years from 2010 until 2015 and there were some incredible memories. There were 40 advisors over 20 years and 20 over 40years and at the time of this printing many are still in the business. What an amazing culture to recruit into. Industry greats like John Horstmann (son John and daughter Kathy), Ron Karabian (son Tim and daughter Sarah), Dennis and Rod Stubblefield, Tom Sommers, Angelo Haddad, and more. What a successful culture! My "marching orders" were to recruit advisors and recruiters and grow the office. We grew to 5 Partners in those 5 years and increased the office production dramatically. My Partners mentored me and helped me develop as a leader. Great leaders like Randy Ladue (past MP in Idaho), Kevin Carano (current MP in Kansas),

Dan Watson (Partner in Bakersfield, now successful advisor), Andrew Schantz (also back in the field) along with the exceptional trainer and my spiritual advisor, Dr. Lyndell Moe, helped me grow as a leader, person, and man.

I went back to Spokane, Washington, "retired" with 3 defined benefit pensions and went back into personal production and my old company (Retirement Nationwide, Inc-which I had founded in 1985). I've been a teacher and coach and wanted to build another team. I accepted a

GA contract in 2019 with another major mutual company. Thanks to RVP David Richert and his boss, Tim Key, for their great service and promises kept. We started the "A-Team" and we're now in 5 states and growing. Thanks especially to my wife Debbie for letting me continue to do what I love to do. Thanks to my sister, Peggy, CPA, 10% owner of the corporation and bookkeeper, videographer, and "bean counter" extraordinaire. Thanks to my number one producer, part owner and one of my successors, Aaron Hill, California Director; Idaho and Washington Director and another successor Kristi Scott, Les Marsh, Montana Director and Noah Taylor, Minnesota Director. Ozzie Knezovich, retired sheriff is the National Director of First Responders and Christopher Wright is one of our best investment advisors. Thanks also to Todd Claypool, Kirk Wald, Jean Jackson (my cousin), Brent Wise, the four wise elders (John Johnson, David Bailey, Dick Branch and Diana Wilhite) and other leaders recruited after this printing and building the A-Team. You guys keep me young and having fun.

It definitely "took a village" to raise me in this great business. I am forever grateful and believe that no one can become successful on their own.

I also couldn't have done this without the gifts, grace and mercy from my Lord and Savior, Jesus Christ. Thanks also to my brother in Christ, Nick McCaskey, my wonderful creative editor of this book and Die Neatly, my first book, 2020. Nick and Amy are truly the definition of servitude and loyalty.

Thanks also to Andy Garrison, who Published this book and Die Neatly in 2020.

Table of Contents

Introduction

In over 40 years in the financial planning business, I can tell you that most people focus on the wrong things. They seek alluring investments and risky ventures that promise big returns. In contrast, this book avoids ever-changing investment advice in favor of timeless, tried-and-true principles of building wealth for most Americans. Specifically, we will look at the three flows of income I dub *living money machines*. These three aspects are the most controllable (and, in some cases most predictable) ways to create the highest-level lifetime income.

A common question people ask of others is, "What do you do for a living?" That question is really asking, "How do you make money?" That second question, though rarely asked out loud, revolves around the subject of you. In other words, making money begins with you. To better explain, let's consider another question.

For years I've asked clients, "What's the largest asset you own?" Over 95% respond with, "My home." They are thinking of assets from a traditional financial perspective, like what you would see on the balance sheet of a set of financial statements. You can supposedly determine your net worth by listing your assets minus your liabilities.

While traditional financial snapshots are important, your largest asset likely isn't your present-day belongings. Rather, it's your human life value. My favorite definition of HLV is: "The present value of your expected future labor income." To get a rough estimate, add up your yearly income or salary and project it over how many years you believe you will work (or earn residual income from your work). If you have decades left to labor and earn money, you are likely worth millions of dollars in expected future labor income.

Thus, especially for a younger person beginning their career, a person's largest asset is their *Human Life Value* (HLV). This means your life, energy, and unique giftings can far exceed material possessions on a balance sheet. Thus, it behooves you to do all that you can to hone yourself and grow your skills to maximize your life, financially and otherwise. This is why the foundation of this book is laid in Part 1, which is all about understanding, growing, and protecting your greatest asset: your HLV.

Two additional *living money machines* are extensions of your Human Life Value and often are large assets at retirement. The first is social security retirement, which grows while you work through the years. Part 2 will discuss social security and strategies for maximizing it in your working years and receiving it at retirement. The second is a defined benefit pension (if you have one), covered in Part 3 of this book. Part 4 is a short section devoted to more advanced post-retirement strategies.

Wisely stewarding your life and growing your potential for your human life value, social security benefits, and defined benefit pensions is the purpose of this book. All three form the foundation for a great retirement. In short, if you get the basics right, you won't need to pursue the latest or hottest investment trends (that usually are very high risk and end in disappointment).

This is why my philosophy on money is called Defensive Financial Planning. It centers around maximizing and protecting your human life value, social security, and pension. Granted, there are other money machines out there. It makes sense to diversify your financial life with real estate, stocks, bonds, annuities, and other income-producing assets. Most of these investments continue forward after you're gone. Those who survive you and take ownership of your accounts (after the IRS perhaps taxes a chunk in taxes) can usually choose to invest more into these accounts if they choose.

What makes the three living money machines discussed in this book unique is that they stop upon your death and cannot be further invested in. Your ability to work naturally ends when you die. Your social security and pensions may transfer to your spouse, but you won't be able to put in more years of work for either. This means you won't accrue more years of service for your pensions or years of wages for social security. Thus, these living money machines are very important to try to maximize while you still are alive and (hopefully) well.

Lastly, please note the important distinction between your financial "offense" and "defense." Like American football, it's advised to have separate advisors for "offense" (investments geared toward wealth accumulation) and "defense" (income replacement, asset protection, and inheritance). In over 40 years, I haven't met one advisor who was an expert in both "offense" and "defense," including me.

Therefore, you need the help of experts in both traditional investments (offense) and what I call protection products (defense). However, this offense and defense approach takes intentionality and resources to build into your life, especially since most financial planners don't specialize in defense.

We'll let other experts in your life help you with your offense. This book aims to help build your defense by learning how to run all three living money machines efficiently as part of your Defensive Financial Planning strategy. I hope to stimulate thought, new challenges, and ideas to help you establish your "defense plan."

PS: If your current adviser is not strong in this defensive approach, give yourself the benefit of hiring an expert in that area too. They will complement one another if they are true professionals. Feel free to reach out to me personally; I want to be a resource for anyone who needs advice at no cost or obligation.

Part 1
Human Life Value

1-A: Introducing Human Life Value

Most people believe their house is their largest asset. Some might say their 401(k). A few will consider their land holdings to be their greatest asset if they own many properties. We've been conditioned to think of financial assets as what we currently have in a bank account or the value on a mortgage statement. Seldom do we think of the truly right answer to our most valuable asset, which has to do with our ability to earn money in the future. Especially for people aged 35 to 55, there is a tremendous ability to earn money for years to come.

This concept of the present value of future earnings is known as *human life value*.[1] It has to do with the adage about giving a person a fish on a single day versus teaching a person to fish for the rest of his or her lifetime. So, if you make $100,000 per year and never got a raise for 30 years, that's $3 million. Using today's dollars, it might be $2.2 million. Regardless, you're worth millions of dollars!

You may own a home worth $400,000 today, which is a wonderful blessing. However, if you have another 20 years to work at a job earning $80,000 a year, you will earn $400,000 in just five years. Even greater, you'll earn over $1,500,000 in the next 20 years.

Suppose you own many pieces of commercial property. That is fantastic, but what is even better is your wisdom and ability to take what you currently have and make new and bigger deals to earn even more. In other words, your ability to make future deals likely outweighs your current on-paper success.

Thus, no matter your bank account size, home value, or investment portfolio, your future human labor is most likely worth far more than

---

[1]   Human Life Value. LifeHappens.org

what you have today. This is why the Introduction to this book dared to make the claim: you are your greatest financial asset. Don't sell yourself short because you are likely worth millions of dollars in terms of Human Life Value (HLV). Indeed, your HLV (the present value of your expected future labor income) depends on many circumstances. Your age and other factors strongly influence your potential earnings.

If you're over age 65, you hopefully already have earned a significant amount of money in your life. Maybe you have built up a 401(k)-retirement account through the decades. Perhaps you are in the minority of people who have a pension. For others less fortunate, your source of income after retirement may be Social Security, which isn't ideal (but is significantly better than nothing). Regardless of your age, it is very beneficial to shift your thinking from present financial assets to a "stream of income" concept.

Your Life as Future Revenue

The importance of future earnings is also akin to the psychological wisdom to compare yourself not to others but to your past self. Try to imagine yourself in the future and how you would want to be. What would it take to become a better person (physically, emotionally, morally, or otherwise) in the next five years? Those improvements are not yet achieved, but they are available to you as long as you stay alive and wisely invest your time into hard work and change.

The same goes for human life value. You can earn and grow your financial situation in ways worth far more than what you likely own today. In accounting terms, there is the notion of future revenue as reported as Accounts Receivable, both short-term and long-term. The idea is that a company is expecting income in the future and is allowed to report this income as an asset on its present-day balance sheet. You also have good things coming to you that you will receive in the future, but most of us don't think of ourselves as storing impending benefits based on what we are doing today.

This book is meant to help shift your thinking to help you live better and more wisely. It is difficult to think of the future, especially to envision good things ahead that we cannot yet see. And yet, preparing now is how we ensure we can walk in greater human life value.

The world has some understanding of the value of our human actions, both presently and in the future. The term "human capital" can be defined as "the economic value of a worker's experience and skills." However, this concept is hard to quantify and no balance sheet in corporate America will ever list a "human capital" line item. And yet, the most important asset for most companies is their individual employees.

There is a famous quote attributed to Henry Ford: *"You can take my factories, burn up my buildings, but give me my people and I'll build the business right back again."* That quote is talking about the future value of people. Even if great hardship is experienced, as long as people retain their ability to function and work hard, the human spirit can fight back from loss and achieve great things. This isn't meant to be a motivational speech, but many people do need a significant shift in their thinking to appreciate just how important their life is, both presently and regarding future potential.

Perhaps now you can see why it is far too limiting to view your house as your largest financial asset. Even large investment accounts with reliable returns cannot match the unique potential for good that each person holds within, both good for the world and good for you and your family financially. Truly, you are your own greatest financial asset, but don't let that go to your head too much. Careful stewarding and guidance from others are required to maximize your human life value.

Calculating Your Human Life Value

Here's a quick table to estimate your Human Life Value. These numbers assume you never get a raise and have an unchanging average income. They also ignore inflation and assume today's dollars are worth the same as tomorrow. Even with such unrealistic assumptions, the point is to quickly see how great your Human Life Value is, based on your estimated income and expected decades of work remaining. For instance, the chart below says a person earning $100,000 who has two more decades to work, has a Human Life Value of $2,000,000.

	Simple *Human Life Value* (HLV)					
	Annual Income ->	**$50,000**	**$100,000**	**$200,000**	**$400,000**	**$1,000,000**
Years of	10	$500,000	$1,000,000	$2,000,000	$4,000,000	$10,000,000
Earnings	20	$1,000,000	$2,000,000	$4,000,000	$8,000,000	$20,000,000
	30	$1,500,000	$3,000,000	$6,000,000	$12,000,000	$30,000,000
	40	$2,000,000	$4,000,000	$8,000,000	$16,000,000	$40,000,000

If you want more precision, there are online calculators to help you determine your potential Human Life Value, such as at LifeHappens. org.[2] Below is a table with ages on the left and annual salaries listed at the top. Find your approximate age and salary to determine your Human Life Value.

	Expected Annual Salary			
Age	**$30,000**	**$50,000**	**$90,000**	**$150,000**
30	$1,378,746	$1,919,542	$2,938,411	$4,203,648
35	$1,198,974	$1,614,433	$2,398,889	$3,378,319
40	$1,078,306	$1,409,194	$2,035,584	$2,622,558
45	$960,314	$1,212,962	$1,692,085	$2,297,093
50	$859,097	$1,047,634	$1,405,843	$1,859,217
55	$774,251	$909,761	$1,166,885	$1,493,673
60	$700,368	$791,232	$963,643	$1,182,766
65	$650,634	$711,444	$826,829	$973,477

Even more precisely, in March 2023, I Googled "highest paid occupations in the US" and found a good article from Jim Probasco[3] showing the average salaries of the top 25 professions provided by the US Bureau of Labor Statistics. I then calculated each career's Human Life Value based on working at that career for 30 years.

---

[2]   Human Life Value Calculator. LifeHappens.org. https://lifehappens.org/human-life-value-calculator/

[3]   25 Highest Paid Occupations in the US. March 2023. https://www.investopedia.com/personal-finance/top-highest-paying-jobs/

Mean Annual Salaries (Higher to Lower)	Annual Salary	Human Life Value (x30)
Cardiologist	$353,970	$10,619,100
Anesthesiologist	$331,190	$9,935,700
Oral and Maxillofacial Surgeon	$311,460	$9,343,800
Emergency Medicine Physician	$310,640	$9,319,200
Orthopedic Surgeon, Except Pediatric	$306,220	$9,186,600
Dermatologist	$302,740	$9,082,200
Radiologist	$301,720	$9,051,600
Surgeon, All Other	$297,800	$8,934,000
Obstetrician-Gynecologist	$296,210	$8,886,300
Pediatric Surgeon	$290,310	$8,709,300
Ophthalmologist, Except Pediatric	$270,090	$8,102,700
Neurologist	$267,660	$8,029,800
Orthodontist	$267,280	$8,018,400
Physician, Pathologists	$267,180	$8,015,400
Psychiatrist	$249,760	$7,492,800
General Internal Medicine Physician	$242,190	$7,265,700
Family Medicine Physician	$235,930	$7,077,900
Physician, All Other	$231,500	$6,945,000
Chief Executive	$213,020	$6,390,600
Nurse Anesthetist	$202,470	$6,074,100
Pediatrician (General)	$198,420	$5,952,600
Airline Pilot, Copilot, and Flight Engineer	$198,190	$5,945,700
Dentist (All Other Specialties)	$175,160	$5,254,800
Dentist (General)	$167,160	$5,014,800
Computer and Information Systems Manager	$162,930	$4,887,900

Now, realistically, most of us won't find ourselves in one of these top-paying professions. That is okay. We need every kind of job, career, and business to make the world function. The purpose of sharing the prior data is to help you think big about your own human life value. Whatever place you are today, you can make a difference. Moreover, you can increase your potential, which is the topic of the next chapter.

Chapter Conclusion

You are blessed with many assets. Some are physical, like a car or maybe a house. Others are your human connections, like your family, parents, siblings, or friendships. Maybe you also have some financial assets, like bank or retirement accounts, investments, and so on. However, I contend that you are your greatest financial asset because you have incredible human life value.

Thus, you are worth investing in today and planning to protect for tomorrow. Take time to consider your worth because you are your greatest financial asset. In the next chapter, we focus on how you can increase your human life value.

1-B: Increasing Human Life Value

Now that you know what Human Life Value is, let's discuss how you can increase it. This is a broad topic because we are talking about becoming more productive. That requires inner motivation, training, discipline, and education.

For starters, education is so important. College graduates tend to earn 84 percent more money than those with only a high school diploma.[4] Proving that you can study and graduate says a lot about you. On the other hand, many young people today are pushed into traditional classroom college when that may not be the best personal path. There is a massive shortage of electricians, plumbers, welders, heating and air conditioning workers, and other such skilled vocations.

Getting training in some 1-year or 2-year vocational schools or apprenticeship programs can be very lucrative and a better fit for many. Moreover, these hardworking professions are what keep society running, including the critically important role of professional truck driving, either local or long-distance trucking professions.

Entrepreneurial paths are also great for many. My own business of life insurance or other sales may be a fit for some. This path still requires much education and training, just not necessarily in a classroom. I often tell the story of Amy, a mother of two young girls in Oregon who had a job in outside sales. She was very good at her work, but the work kept pushing her to travel further and further away from home on many days. She worked very hard and was personable and smart. She told me to keep in touch the first time I tried to recruit her onto my team.

---

[4]   How does a college degree improve graduates' employment and earnings potential? APLU.org. https://www.aplu.org/our-work/4-policy-and-advocacy/publicuvalues/employment-earnings/

About a year later, I called her. She was once again far from home. She said she hated her job and asked me, "When can I start?" Once she began, she wrote over 100 life insurance cases every year and got promoted to partner quickly. Around that same time, she had a friend, Lorraine, who was a single parent in a small town of about 20,000 people on the Oregon coast. That friend got into the business and also wrote 100 cases for the first couple of years and got promoted. These two were pillars in my organization for years earning mid-six-figure incomes in the early 2000s. What a blessing it was to mentor these two professionals and see their families be richly rewarded and increase their HLV.

What matters is that you evaluate your life and try to determine what is best aligned with your passions and skills. Then you can design a realistic plan for what is available to you in the next couple of years, five years, and beyond. In today's world, it is not uncommon for people to go back to vocational school or college to retrain for another profession.

It would be ideal if we all got excellent guidance and training from our parents when we grew up. One of the roles of parents is to carefully study their children and strongly support a child's natural strengths while trying to shore up weaknesses. Rather than push children down a certain path, every child has a unique path that is likely best for them. Unfortunately, most of us don't get such dedicated and focused guidance from our parents. Thus, it falls to many of us after entering adulthood to try to evaluate our own lives and find what life-purpose best matches our true giftings.

Lifetime Learning

Despite the different paths we can take, the central theme is one of building a strong work ethic that doesn't cut your potential short. Again, by potential, we can quantify it using human life value. Young people sometimes quit their education and training and "settle for" careers too early and end up with a lot less Human Life Value than they could achieve.

If you have 30 to 40 years to work, get excited about your Human Life Value potential. Too many view their working years as drudgery or a chore. A change in mindset is the first step in increasing your human life value. Get positive about your potential and think about what you can earn. Work 30 years and average $200,000 per year and $6,000,000 will be your earned income. What a blessing to be able to work and potentially earn so much. Maybe that figure seems out of reach, but you are reading this book to help you think and aim bigger.

Simply put, far too many people don't quantify their human life value. Don't go through life on autopilot, putting in your hours year after year without reflection. Make it a sort of game to evaluate yourself each year regarding HLV. What new skills have you learned to increase your HLV? Have you 'leveled up' this year by getting a raise, beginning a training program, taking college classes, starting a side business, or overcoming bad habits or vices?

If you're dissatisfied with your place in life, start changing your life by writing down and talking about the potential changes you can make to get you to where you want to be. If you're fortunate to be passionate about your present employment or career, continue to find ways to maximize your income through education, training, negotiations, and the pursuit of other side opportunities.

A Personal Take

When I was new in the life insurance business (back in 1983), there was a philosophy we would teach clients that some have gotten away from. The statement was "You'll earn a fortune." It was accompanied by a similar career earnings table (but with smaller numbers back then). I was making less than $30,000 a year as a high school physics teacher, but I did the math. I figured if I earned an average of $50,000 a year for 30 years, my total earnings would be $1.5 million. So even though my wife and I had two kids and a small home, I knew that the potential was there for the "fortune" that I'd earn in the future.

With my untapped fortune in mind, I continued my education and obtained my master's degree in education administration. This education would not only allow me to make more income, but I would have a bigger pension. With my wife being a homemaker (the most important job in the world), I sold Real Estate from 1978 to 1982. Some would look at the Real Estate side business as simply a way to earn more money in the here and now, but I had the long view in mind. I saw the extra business as a way to increase my Human Life Value and grow my "fortune" of a lifetime.

I loved selling Real Estate. We sold our home and bought a bigger one with acreage. This space was used to start Lusk Quarter Horses as another side business. All was well until mortgage interest rates skyrocketed to 15 to 18% in 1981 and 1982. Real Estate sales tanked. We were financially distraught with savings depleted and credit cards maxed out. I knew I had to change careers to support our lifestyle, or my wife would have to sell the horses and work "outside the home." After much prayer and discussion, I boldly joined the financial planning industry. I focused on selling life insurance and disability income protection.

This business is not for everyone, but it has been an incredible blessing to our family. I have built substantially more Human Life Value than I would have otherwise, and I have the satisfaction of helping thousands of people. Had the Real Estate market not tanked, I would've moved into education administration like many of my friends and clients and who have retired from the Washington State Teacher's Retirement System with lifetime pension income. Such a defined benefit pension is another living money machine and the entire focus of Part 3 of this book.

Teaching and coaching are callings, and you'll never be paid what you're worth. However, the impact you make on future living money machines (your students) can't be quantified. Those who teach are truly allowing others to increase their human life value, which makes the world a better place for all of us. The same goes for many other public servant professions. You perhaps will earn less money than in the private sector, but you are doing critical work for the world. Whether in the forest service, the postal service, or as a police or firefighter, another major benefit to you is the possible lifetime defined benefit pension. Not everyone qualifies, depending on your role. If you do qualify, many Federal agencies and every state have defined benefit pensions that pay you for life. The longer you work in the public sector and the more money you make each year, the bigger your pension will be. Again, see Part 3 of this bo

Careers and Raises

Why is it so important to study and learn and grow your Human Life Value? Education is power. It has the largest impact on developing your Human Life Value. Consider the following chart of salaries and raises.

30-Year Career "Real Raises" 2/25/23				
Starting Salary	$60,000			
Raise Percents	3% Raises	4% Raises	5% Raises	6% Raises
10	$80,635	$88,815	$97,734	$107,451
20	$108,367	$131,467	$159,198	$192,428
30	$145,636	$194,604	$259,317	$344,609
30 Years Total	$3,000,161	$3,559,700	$4,245,647	$5,088,101
Average	$100,000	$119,000	$142,000	$170,000

Starting Salary	$120,000			
Raise Percents	3% Raises	4% Raises	5% Raises	6% Raises
10	$161,270	$172,629	$195,467	$214,902
20	$216,733	$262,935	$318,396	$384,856
30	$291,271	$387,208	$518,633	$689,214
30 Years Total	$6,000,321	$7,119,400	$8,491,295	$10,176,201
Average	$200,000	$237,000	$283,000	$339,000

Takeaways:

You will see that I love tracking data and making 'games' of otherwise dull activities. For instance, track your raises every year. Try to beat your prior raises and 'outdo' yourself year after year. Study how your job's pay scale works. Are there new opportunities at your current company or in your present career?

We have already spoken of the importance of education. Some education will directly boost your earnings, especially at some government jobs. Get advanced degrees that fit your field of work. Get more certifications. Study topics that you simply love to spark your creativity. Invest in your hobbies. It may sound strange but take your relaxation seriously. I love woodworking and making baseball bats, bowls, and furniture for my family and friends. That isn't about increasing my Human Life Value, but even leisure activities let us recharge so we can be our best in our professional work lives.

Professional Sales

Many people dislike salespeople and would in no way even consider such an endeavor for themselves. However, I wish more people would see sales in a positive light. The process of selling products and services is essential to our world. Think of your favorite goods and technologies. Someone sold those products to businesses, and then the businesses sold those products to you. And it's a great thing someone is selling because you and I would certainly be in trouble if nobody was offering to sell us food, beverages, bandages, plates, utensils, and so much more. What about plumbing repairs and new furnaces and so on? Without sales, we'd be forced to barter and trade and have significantly worse lives.

Sales is also a wonderful gateway out of the rut of paycheck-to-paycheck living. It is a way to earn more based on your effort versus someone's opinion of your value. As much as the sales profession gets a bad rap, who enjoys having a boss or corporation determine when you can leave your desk, use the bathroom, or run an errand for your family? Many sales careers give you the flexibility to earn a living while still living out your desired schedule.

Sales is also wonderfully fair. It is a numbers game. If you have a quality product, there will be people out there who will want to buy it. Hence, you can understand that along with the rejection of many will come the business of plenty of others. If you put in the work, you will succeed. If you're a "people person", that opportunity is a real blessing for people feel that they are stuck in 'dead-end' jobs.

I'm a baseball mega-fan. I played in college, semi-pros, and then 15 years of fast-pitch softball. Even the best hitters in baseball don't break the 40% success rate. In fact, in 2023, only nine hitters in Major League Baseball hit over a .300 batting average at the end of the season (3 of out of 10 times at the plate, equaling 30% success). The average salary of those nine was almost $17 million per year. Not a bad 'gig' when you can fail at your job 70% of the time!

Actually, a 70% miss rate isn't failing because swinging and missing is part of your job. You just have to practice hard, show up, and then take a chance to hit the ball. This is the same philosophy of sales. You get on a great team, practice hard, reach out, and make the pitch. You will certainly "swing and miss" many times, but that is a necessary part of the sales 'game.' You'll hit just enough times to eventually score a "home run" for you and your family.

I've been in the life insurance sales business for over 40 years. What I love about the life insurance business is how extremely predictable it is. It is such a scientific, predictable business. It doesn't depend on interest rates, the success of the economy, market downturns, or otherwise. Even through the Covid pandemic, people still needed (perhaps more so) what life insurance could do for them. But it's not retail. People rarely wake up and say, "Hey, let's go shopping for life insurance today." You must believe you have what people need and bring the opportunity to them.

I use the time-tested sales ratio of 10-3-1. "For every 10 qualified individuals you put into your "funnel," 3 will become prospects (complete a needs analysis with you) and 1 will buy (become a client)." – Al Granum, General Agent, Northwest Mutual. I like the 10-3-1 ratio because it's the same percentage as two baseball batting averages of .300. Three out of 10 will meet with me, which is 30%. Then 1 out of 3 (30%) of these will buy. That means I only need 1 out of 10 attempts to be successes to be doing as well in life insurance as the top professional baseball players in the world.

With this 10-3-1 ratio, all I have to do is generate enough activity to drive my success. If I keep meeting with enough new people, I will be successful. This has worked amazingly for me and hundreds of other advisors that I have recruited and trained over my many decades. Take the emotion and rejection out of the equation and simply work the numbers. (For more on this, read Die Neatly.)

Many other sales careers work the same way. You have the ability in sales to far outperform what value is placed on your earnings with wages and salaries. They all have core principles in common with each other and with those of us in the financial services industry. They are hard workers who believe in their product, know how to manage and push through rejection, are goal-oriented, and love to help people be better off than before they showed up.

For other professional sales, such as some retail jobs, you might have a salary plus commissions. This gives you some "breathing room" and security from the salary, but the commissions piece is the real method of accelerating your human life value. My advice is to "shatter" any quota that the company puts in front of you. Then, you will always in a position of strength when the economy changes and layoffs come. Operate in "front of the pack," be competitive, and win those bonuses and trips. Have fun, too, and become a "master salesperson" because the world will always need trustworthy and hardworking salespeople.

Still, everyone is different. A sales career isn't right for everyone. Many people I know have no desire to "put themselves out there" in the world of professional sales. My wife is one of these people who simply doesn't click with sales. That's okay. She has so many other incredible talents and giftings that she has used to massively bless others. Certainly, we need people in all professions and life callings. Not everyone will do sales, or nursing, or accounting, or construction, but where would the world be without each of us following our unique passions?

I would ask you not to prejudge any profession because you might miss out on your true calling. For sales, especially, it might not be what you think it is. I often say, "Nothing in our economy moves without some product being sold." Those of you who own your own business know how important marketing, sales, and promotional efforts are to the success of your business. So, if you've never considered or tried out a flexible sales job like life insurance, at least consider it as a way to increase your human life value. You might even enjoy it!

Saving versus Spending

The prior half of this chapter was about actively growing our Human Life Value through personal improvement. The goal, in short, is to make more money. However, how much you earn is only half the picture of a healthy financial life. The other half is less glamorous: how much you spend. I'm sure we've all known people who have made a bunch of money only to spend it all and go into debt. I'll share my own story in a moment because I've been one of these people. Maybe you have too.

Remember how I said vocations can be a lucrative field? There was a young college man who worked the summer as a plumber's apprentice for his dad's plumbing business. This young man earned thousands upon thousands of dollars in just a couple of months. He came back to college bragging about his summer job, but soon he had spent it all. Where did the money go? Entertainment products, a big screen TV, DVDs, and other things. Earning all that money is great, but you don't want to set yourself for the "earn big, spend even bigger" mentality that is so tempting.

We live in a society of "immediate gratification." Whether it's a new car, birthday presents, bonuses, dinners out, nice clothes, vacations, and the list goes on and on. As children and adults in America (and other affluent nations), we "want it now." I'm as guilty as the majority. I used to say, "If they sold college degrees, I'd borrow money to buy one." It has taken me many years to try and conquer this "must have it now" mentality and desire.

I do admit to "marrying up" with my wife. She is a world-class saver, bargain shopper, and evaluator of every purchase. Whether it's 2-for-1 sandwich offers, car deals, airline ticket specials, or something else, she has always looked for a good deal over our nearly 50 years of marriage. I wasn't always so careful with spending. Way back, I argued with her as I maxed out a couple of credit cards, financed a new car, and lost money on stocks and business ventures. It turns out she was right, and my mentality was the problem. I was earning a lot of money, but like many young professionals, I wasn't financially disciplined. I thought making money meant I could spend what I wanted and struggled to keep a good share of what I made. People speak of "take-home" pay. But what good does it do you to take it home and then have it walk right out the door? Such was my case, as a "world-class spender." Plus, I had a much too high tolerance for debt. It just didn't bother me.

Although my wife was right, others gave me bad advice. A veteran financial advisor once told me, "Just borrow your way out of debt." That may sound weird and counter-intuitive to most rational people, but when you grow up poor and then finally make good money, you never have enough, so borrowing more is very tempting. Plus, if you're "a spender," it makes total sense. It's all about cash flow, right? No!

Lessons from My Story

In 2005, I was almost $1 million in debt, with $500,000 of that as unsecured debt and the other $500,000 as my mortgage. My wife would say, "You're a Certified Financial Planner and you are a hypocrite." She was right yet again. I finally got tired of being at odds with my wife about my spending habits. I finally promised her to reduce our debt. I thankfully paid off all our debt (except our mortgage) over about five years of sacrifice, prayer, and commitment. That was a $100,000 reduction per year of unsecured debt!

This was the hardest, yet most satisfying financial growth I've ever accomplished. I had to resist urges and endure "deferred gratification." I also had to have faith that being a better steward of money would bring blessings to me, my family, and those around me. Most of all, I had to prove to myself and my wife that I could follow through with what I said I was going to do. In the meantime, my income kept increasing as I reduced the debt, so my lifestyle increased.

Rewards have come. I get more respect from my wife and family. More investments are available to me. I have more reserves to face unexpected challenges and bless others who experience sudden hardships. I can also better enjoy my income, especially my pensions, social security, and immediate annuities that are guaranteed for life. It feels great to only have a very manageable mortgage payment.

Why do I share my personal story of debt and financial victory? I believe there are two ways we learn best:

1. **By our mistakes** (don't do what I did).

2. **By the mistakes of others** (learn from others who have gone before you).

If you also struggle with debt, overspending, and immediate gratification, please let my story help change your life. Your family will thank you, even if you disappoint the siren song of the advertisers who say, "Buy today, pay later." It's so much better to put yourself in a position of blessing, springing forth from good decisions today. Now, in my present life, I find myself in the reaping many blessings, for myself and others. My life mission is to help people and advisors become better "savers" and resist "borrowing to spend."

In other words, today I can be a hypocrisy-free financial coach. If you'll allow me, I want to coach you to do the following.

1. Complete an estate plan (will or trust) with a good attorney. (We're all one heartbeat from eternity.)

2. Provide adequate protection for your family in the event of premature death or disability. (Have a defensive financial specialist help you determine your "replacement income" amount.)

3. Save money "until it hurts" (see the Savings 101 chart below).

Save Until It Hurts

I've used this "save until it hurts" saying and taught many clients and advisors over decades, and that there's no refuting it. I will add context: I don't mean hurts as in "break your arm." It's more like physical stretching: push yourself until you feel it but don't cause lasting harm. For example, if you're in a very tight spot financially, you may need to spend most of your money on bills and essential life items like food. In this scenario, how you save will look different. You can still save in creative ways such as using coupons and finding excellent values (like my wife excels in doin). However, if you have more breathing room, putting, say, $200 a month in a savings account may not hurt at all. In this case, push yourself further. Again, it's much like sports training. At first, you begin carefully and can't do too much. Later, you require much more strenuous activity. Likewise, save as much as you can up to the point you start to feel it. Easy? No way. Life changing? Always.

If you're a saver (also like my wife), this is no problem. Ideally, we all are raised right and taught to save money as young children. This was my wife's case. As a young girl, she built up a collection of several dozen John F. Kennedy silver half-dollars (she still has them to this day—how's that for lifetime savings?). Sadly, most of us didn't get nurtured and guided into wise financial decision-making from childhood, and saving money is tough for nearly everyone. Plus, for many of us, spending is a sort of addiction. It's okay to admit that you have a problem and need help like I needed for many years.

What are some suggestions to help you get started? Try for "improvement, not perfection." When I was paying off my $500,000 of unsecured debt, my wife was not impressed until about three years into the process. I don't blame her. She'd heard enough of my empty promises and excuses and feared I would "relapse" into my old spending habits. As I said, I needed a lot of help and had to "stick with the plan" even when the "buying impulse" came many times!

I still failed a few times, especially with my desire to have new cars. I compromised and bought cars that were two to three years old for half the cost. I drove them to over 100,000 miles, which was hard for someone who has created a pattern of "new stuff" for years. But I was improving and okay with not being perfect on my road to a better financial mentality.

Suggestions to Become a Better Saver

1. **Live within your means.** Too bad our federal government doesn't follow this principle. Instead, it keeps printing money. You can't do that, so you shouldn't follow their example. The famous Wayne Cotton, CFP said, "If your outgo exceeds your income, then your upkeep will be your downfall."

2. **Pay yourself first.** The exception to this rule is if you tithe or give to charity. Do that first if you are so moved, but the next priority is setting aside money for your future needs. Create a budget (that's right, a BUDGET) to help you determine how much you can save each month.

3. **Take 50% of every raise and invest it.** Put half of your raises into after-tax investments and accumulation that grows tax deferred, that you can withdraw tax-free. The other two instruments are ROTH IRAs and LIRPs (see the Saving 101 diagram-The Three Legged Stool).

4. **Take 75% windfalls (gifts, inheritances, bonuses, etc.) and do the same as #3**. It's tough to put away so much money, but you can still make good use of the 25% remaining in creative ways.

5. **Save then purchase.** Avoid high-interest credit cards or debt for major purchases. Emergencies happen, but if you follow the prior four steps, you likely will have a good reserve saved up when you need it.

6. **Pay off unsecured or depreciating asset debt.** I recommend starting with the highest interest rate debt first (sometimes called the avalanche method). But some people encourage you to start with the smallest balance first (the snowball method) and then take that payment amount and "snowball" it into the next smallest balance's monthly payment.[5] Either way, make a detailed plan and stick to it.

7. **Don't pay off your mortgage if it is at a low interest rate.** If you are blessed with a low interest rate mortgage, it is often wiser to use your money for things other than making extra principal payments on your mortgage. For instance, pay off all your other debt first, as noted above. Build your savings account balance to 3 to 6 times your current monthly income (6 months of reserves or more is great). Find savings accounts and investment vehicles that earn a higher interest rate than your mortgage, even tax-advantaged options. On a personal note, at age 66, I refinanced our mortgage at 2.625% for 30 years, which was a great way to use LEVERAGED DEBT—see that section in this book. Every situation is unique. For me, at a 2.625% interest rate, it didn't make sense for me to pay any extra toward my mortgage when I could get 7-10% earnings or better elsewhere. This is an example of using "leveraged debt" to make more money.

---

[5] Comparing the snowball and the avalanche methods of paying down debt. Retrieved 9/4/2023. https://www.wellsfargo.com/goals-credit/smarter-credit/manage-your-debt/snowball-vs-avalanche-paydown/

8. **Consider a second business or career.** If you still want more money than you're able to earn, look at a separate business or new career. To keep up with my spending and lifestyle, I had to do both early in my married life.

9. **Teach your kids to save money.** If you pay them allowances, give them gifts, or otherwise have them receive money, use the ten-thirty-thirty-thirty rule. A great balanced plan means you teach your kids to donate 10%, spend 30%, save 30% for things you want to get in the next 6 months to two years, and save 30% for long-term needs.

10. **Track your net worth yearly.** Your net worth is your assets (what you own) minus liabilities (what you owe). Even if you're starting a new career with tens of thousands of student loan debt and are "upside down" financially (liabilities greater than assets), write it all down and compare your position at the start of the year to the end of the year. This gives you a better understanding of your financial life and motivates you to improve your position month after month, year after year. Winners keep score! Personally, even when my debt was over $1,000,000, I still had a positive net worth. Nevertheless, that situation was embarrassing since I had a debt-to-asset ratio greater than 40%. Today that ratio is under 10%, and my only debt (my mortgage) is "working for me" (leveraged).

11. **Have an accountability partner.** This person can be your spouse, financial adviser, sibling, etc. Getting to a better place financially is too hard to do alone. Even if you're a natural saver, having another person give you a fresh perspective is very helpful.

12. **Invest in your human life value.** Education, training, skills, and other self-improvement programs will help make you more marketable in this economy (and all future economies).

Good Debt versus Bad Debt

You can't be a good saver and not manage, reduce, and eventually eliminate "bad debt." I define "bad debt" as higher interest unsecured debt or debt secured by depreciating assets (vehicles, boats, RVs, etc.). We want "it" and don't have the money, so we finance it. I admit that this is a problem for me. It is hard to resist the allure of new things, especially new cars. Resisting is easier for me when I think about less of my budget going to debt service if I don't buy the thing. When it's unsecured debt, it becomes a vacuum, sucking money out of your bank with usually nothing to show for it.

Leveraged Debt

The other type of debt is "good debt," also known as leveraged debt. This means the debt acts as a multiplier, letting you do things you wouldn't be able to do otherwise to build your financial life. It is debt that helps you build your life and finances. For instance, your mortgage can be a type of leveraged debt, assuming you purchased your home wisely. Hopefully, you didn't buy more than you could afford, and it is best if you have great credit and can get a lower-interest loan. It also helps to buy at the right time when the real estate market isn't inflated and overpriced. Even if you had outside forces working against you, over time, a home can still be "good debt."

Let me explain "leveraged debt." First, I'm not talking about the traditional definition of leverage in the financial world. In that space, leverage is a term that means taking on debt and then investing it to multiply your potential returns. This can be very risky, akin to high-stakes gambling: big risk, big reward. Here is what I mean by "leveraged debt." It is debt usually secured by real estate. Most of the wealthiest people in the world have a large portion of their assets invested in real estate (especially commercial properties) and "leverage the growth" by having mortgages on those real estate assets.

One of the key ownerships my wife and I have had in almost 50 years of marriage is six homes over the years. We've made substantial money on five out of the six properties. We had to sell the other property at a loss when my job required a transfer across the country while working for a major life insurance company. Fortunately, the company paid extra money to us through an incredible moving compensation package in 2010 when the market was down. The market was also down in our new location, so we got to buy low and came out ahead 5 years later when we sold it.

On average over the last 50 years, real estate has outperformed the stock market and should continue to do so. Therefore, it is highly advisable to build a real estate portfolio that includes a personal home, rental house, and even commercial real estate. The problem is that most of us don't have hundreds of thousands (or millions) of dollars lying around to buy properties.

Leverage uses the concept of OPM (other people's money). It lets us put down 10-20% of the purchase price. The bank, mortgage company, or private party lends us the balance. The downside is that we must pay back that borrowed money with interest. However, if I can buy a property that will appreciate at a better rate than the interest rate I pay on my mortgage, then I make money in the end. That's leverage! Like a crowbar or shovel, we make an effort, but the impact (power) is multiplied by using the right tool in the right way at the right time.

Your Home: How Much to Borrow

So, how much should you borrow to buy a home? I recommend getting advice from a qualified mortgage lender and getting "prequalified" for a home worth a value up to "X." Don't get your heart broken by looking for homes out of your price range and making an offer only to find out your income and credit score disqualify you. A good mortgage lender can also help you increase your credit score over time to get a better interest rate and financing. This may also take some "deferred gratification" to find the right time to buy, based on the market, prevailing interest rates and your financial situation.

I like to put the least amount down. That may be controversial to some. If you're a military veteran, you can qualify for a VA loan with little down, but there are up-front VA loan costs, etc. Again, your mortgage lender can be a great resource here, along with wise financial advisers.

Buying a home, especially your first home, can be a very rewarding and exhilarating time. Certainly, home ownership gives you more control and choices. You may wish to defer that dream and focus on eliminating much of your "bad debt" first, though.

One of my favorite questions to ask homeowners in an appreciating market (like the years of 2019-2022), is this: "How much will you make on your mortgage next year if your home appreciates at 8% and your mortgage is 4%? Most people look at me with a funny face and say, "Zero." Several realtors, mortgage lenders, and financial planners also flunked this same question when I asked them. Please review the diagram below.

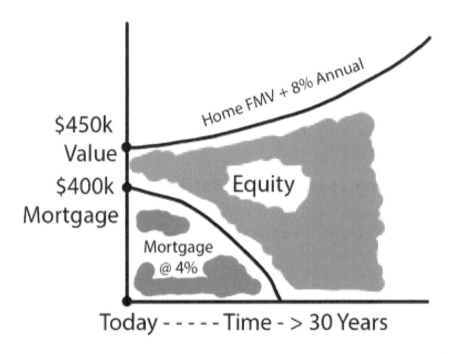

Notice that the FMV (fair market value) of the home increases over time. Our diagram estimates the increase at 8% annually. The mortgage reduces, but it's not a straight line. This is because mortgages have interest front-loaded through a formula known as amortization. This is why banks make so much money on mortgages. The borrower always pays the largest amount of interest upfront. Look at any amortization schedule and you'll see that there are only small principal reductions in the first few years. Most of your monthly payment goes to interest.

Eventually, you reach a point where you are paying more toward principal than toward interest. With a 4%, 30-year mortgage, the payment (P&I) would be $1,910 per month. $1,333 of this goes toward interest in the first month. Even after 5 years (60 payments totaling $114,600), you still owe $362,491 on a $400,000 original mortgage, and you paid $76,370 in total interest. In 10 years (120 payments totaling $229,200), you still owe $315,992 and paid $144,295 in total interest.

The Return on Your Mortgage

These cold, hard numbers would be very depressing if you didn't realize a couple of things. First, you got the benefit of living in your home for those 5 to 10 years. Hopefully, you enjoyed years of making great memories in your home. Second, in those same 5 to 10 years, your equity has exploded because of the 8% increased property value on average each year. Therefore, despite paying so much interest on your mortgage, your home is an excellent investment. That's LEVERAGE. See the following table.

Year	Home FMV*	Mortgage*	Equity*	Growth	Rate of Return
0	$450,000	$400,000	$50,000	--	--
5	$661,000	$362,000	$299,000	43.00%	17%
10	$972,000	$315,000	$657,000	29.40%	13%
*Rounded to the nearest thousand dollars					

With the $1,910 monthly payment (ignoring taxes, insurance, and closing costs), you would have to earn over 13% in an investment account to reach a $657,000 value in 10 years. You might be able to pick the right stocks to get that rate of return, but historically the stock market grows at 9-10% over any 10-year period.

Where does this leverage come from? Go back to the diagram. The answer to the question, "How much will you make on your mortgage?" is 4% (8%-4%). It's just math. You made 8% on the appreciation of the FMV of your home: $450,000 value x 8% = $36,000. Realize that you make 8% on the entire value (FMV), not just the equity. So, you paid $22,920 in PI (principal & interest: $1,910 per month times 12 years) that first year to make $36,000. Plus, you reduced your mortgage by about $7,000. Your net worth already looks better.

If you itemized your tax return, you could also take most of your mortgage interest as a tax deduction. Except for business debt, this is the only deductible personal interest in the current tax code (year 2022). That may be an advantage to consider.

Rentals and commercial real estate also have the advantage of deduction for depreciation of the buildings. With the interest deduction, depreciation, and capital improvements, the rental income can create a positive cash flow with your leveraged debt. Be careful here, though, because vacancies, bad tenants, and maintenance expenses can really hurt that cash flow and even damage your property.

When I was a landlord, I often was too nice and empathized too much with tenants who were late or skipped their rent and wanted to take advantage of my kindness. However, I have several clients who are experts in residential and commercial real estate, and their financial portfolio is made up, in large part, of such real estate. Before you try this yourself, I'd do a joint venture with someone you trust who is already experienced in real estate investing.

The Three-Legged Stool

For decades, we developed the philosophy of diversified savings of 15-21% of your income into balanced "legs" of a three-legged stool. The legs are "Short-Term," "Mid-Term," and "Long-Term."

The idea is that you concurrently plan for your immediate needs (and emergencies), upcoming desires like education and business opportunities, and much longer-term retirement goals. To achieve a good balance, you put 5-7% into each leg until you reach the limits of each leg. The suggested limits are as follows.

- Short-Term: 3-6 months, 25-50% of Income

- Mid-Term: After 3-6 months in leg 1, put excess here

- Long-Term: Maximize up to the retirement account match (take the free money)

Again, put any excess in the middle leg with tax-free access. See the diagram below:

Why Put the Excess into Tax-Free Accounts?

In the world we live in today, too many people are trying to "save taxes" today by overfunding their 401(k) plan or Traditional IRA. By "overfunding" I mean going above any 401(k) match or 7% (the lower of the two). You're not saving taxes by doing this. You're deferring them. If tax rates are higher in the future (which I'm convinced they will be— read David McKnight's, *The Power of Zero*), you will pay a higher rate in taxes down the road on that same money. Please read the book and study this.

A 401(k) plan is a great instrument to accumulate tax-deferred assets, and you should certainly "maximize" contributions up to your employer's match. However, above the match, you need to factor in future tax rates. If you honestly believe you'll be in a lower tax bracket in the future (at retirement age), then fund your 401(k) plan above the match. If, however, you think (as I do) that tax rates will be much higher in the future, then overfund the middle leg. Pay taxes on the "seed" so you can enjoy the "harvest" free of taxes later. The two instruments in this middle leg are a ROTH IRA and a LIRP (Life Insurance Retirement Plan).

Top 1% Earners

For very high-income earners (top 1%), these stool leg ratios are even more important. Fortune Magazine in a July 2023 report labeled the top 1% of wage earners at over $650,000 per year. These successful earners are not only in the highest income tax bracket but will probably always be. With that in mind, the middle leg of our stool is even more important. Unfortunately, such earners make too much money to qualify for a ROTH IRA. Thus, a LIRP becomes even more important.

They also don't need 50% in liquid assets (leg one). Usually, no one needs more than $75,000 to $100,000 in cash unless you are putting money on the "sidelines," trying to carefully time the purchase of an investment opportunity. Don't store too much money in low-yield accounts. Put your money in better-yielding investments with tax advantages.

They might want more in the third leg, but as David McKnight, the author of The Power of Zero, points out, any amount that RMDs (required minimum distributions) would be greater than the standard deduction should look at ROTH Conversions. This means moving qualified money to a ROTH and paying the taxes for this year to "remove the IRS" from future taxation. This is called a "backdoor ROTH."

Many employees have added a ROTH contribution option for their 401(k) plan whereby you don't have to be concerned about the income limits and contribution limits of individual ROTHs and can contribute up to $25,000/year (in 2024, subject to increases with inflation). The "match" from the employer can't be "Rothified" (after tax, and TAX-FREE at retirement) as it is a business deduction and is therefore taxable to the employee during the distribution phase. The employee's contribution isn't deductible (the employee decides to pay taxes on the "Seed" versus the "harvest") for the ROTH 401(k).

So, between the ROTH conversion, ROTH 401(k) plan, and a well-structured LIRP, there are many tax-wise accumulation devices to plan for future higher marginal tax rates.

Example: An executive is making $1,000,000 per year and is concerned about future rising tax rates. She is age 50, healthy, and has over $1.5 million already in her pre-tax 401(k) plan. She has little debt, two grown kids, and two awesome grandkids, whom she loves to spoil. Her husband is a teacher making $100,000 and has a state teacher's retirement plan. They have no will or trust.

Suggestions to consider:

1. Make sure to meet with a qualified estate planning attorney and set up appropriate wills/trusts, health care directives, and durable powers of attorney.

2. Max out the ROTH 401(k) contributions of $23,00/year and increase to the limit each year.

3. Do NOT contribute to any state 403(b) teacher's retirement account for her husband as there is already too much tax-qualified money ($1.5 million in her 401(k)). (Again, refer to The Power of Zero book.) If he is contributing to a 403(b) account (TSA or TDA for educators and nonprofit organizations), he should stop and, if insurable, build a powerful LIRP so he can "maximize his pension" (see Chapter 3-B on increasing defined benefit pensions).

4. She should consider putting $150,000-$200,000 into a LIRP and fund it for 10 years. This will generate enormous leverage and 25 or more years of tax-free income at retirement.

5. The two of them should consider gifting $34,000 (max annual gift exclusion in 2023, see gift splitting[6]) to each child and grandchild. This money can also accumulate in a trust if needed. LIRPs on my grandchildren are one of my favorite places to move money. Your financial advisor, accountant, and attorney should be included to help you here.

6. This couple should review their life insurance, long-term care insurance, and disability income protection on a regular (at least annual) basis.

7. They should work with only credentialed advisors with a CFP, CLU, or ChFC who will personalize their plan to meet their changing needs.

Chapter Conclusion

There are many ways to improve your ability to earn money. Traditional education is the most obvious, but investing in specific certifications, trade schools, or vocational training can also be incredibly valuable. Don't sell yourself short by settling for a job or career you don't love (and doesn't pay well). My own story involves going to school and college, starting businesses, and switching to my financial advisor career. Even in my career, I've purposefully worked at multiple companies to maximize my earnings and pensions (covered in Part 3). There are many great careers out there, and no matter where you are at, you can better yourself. Often, you are the only one who will fight for what you're worth.

In conjunction with increasing your human life value, you also want to become a wise spender and saver. Spend money when you need to but learn to save until it hurts. I shared my story as an example of what not

---

6   Planning strategies for gift splitting. Fidelity. Retrieved 9/7/2023. https://www.fidelity.com/learning-center/wealth-management-insights/gift-splitting

to do in your early years. Thankfully, I got things together later in life, but you can start smart savings and spending habits today.

A big part of wise spending is knowing the difference between good and bad debt. We all know not to rack up credit card debt, but also beware of any debt not secured by an appreciating asset. On the other hand, your mortgage can be a good form of debt that even helps you build wealth.

In the end, you want to build a solid three-legged stool approach to saving money, based on your short-, mid-, and long-term financial needs. You certainly can't plan for all events but being mindful with your money leads to great returns. Also make sure to 'tax-diversify' your wealth accumulation. Please read The Power of Zero by David McKnight. If you want a free copy, contact us for a consultation.

The next chapter covers the big financial hits you can't always avoid, so let's move on to protecting your largest asset.

1-C: Protecting Your Largest Asset

The prior two chapters introduced Human Life Value and discussed how to increase it. Ideally, every person would be raised in a loving home, get good guidance, start a career, continue learning and growing, retire successfully, and then live in good health until passing away peacefully at age 90 or so. However, life rarely goes so smoothly. There are no guarantees that you will have good health or even stay alive through the decades.

In my book, *Die Neatly,*[7] I spoke of two major events that can suddenly destroy or eviscerate your Human Life Value. Those events are: premature death and disability. Both are probably low probability today but catastrophic financially is they happen. Especially if you are younger, you could lose millions of dollars in expected future earnings if you become disabled. Your family could also lose it all if you die unexpectedly. Please understand there is so much at stake, so protect your human life value.

Money Machines (Adapted from Die Neatly)

To better understand why we must protect our human life value, let me introduce the "money machine" concept. To explain, allow me to have some fun with a fantastic story.

Let's say that you are 20 years old and have heard of a special festival coming to your town. The festival promises to change people's lives. Unsure about your direction in life, you decide to go. One day at the festival, you see an intriguing tent that seems to contain a shop you've

---

[7]   Die Neatly. Jim Lusk. 2020. (Copies also available upon request. See www.retirementnationwide.com.)

never heard of before. As you enter the tent, the shop owner, a wise old sage, tells you he has a special item for you only. He brings out a machine, about the size of a breadbox that looks like the merging of an ATM and a toaster. The shop owner informs you that it is calibrated to work only with your unique retinal scan and voice activation. You are dubious, so you ask how it works. It's quite simple: at the start of each month, you put your fingerprint on it for further verification and then it spits out $5,000 for you to use however you like. Every single month it will do this for you, like a kind of magic. He calls it a Money Machine.

This Money Machine seems too good to be true. What's the catch? The man informs you that there are no replaceable parts, and you can never get issued another one. This is a truly once-in-a-lifetime product that will work if you properly maintain and operate it. So, how much will you pay for that machine? $5,000 per month is $60,000 per year. Over 40 years is $2.4 million. However, the shop owner isn't going to charge you millions for it. In fact, he says it is his gift to you, free of charge. You gladly take it and clutch the Money Machine very carefully to your body, so as not to drop or damage it.

Moreover, the Money Machine tent seems to have vanished. You get the feeling you have been gifted something of extreme importance. There is no going back, and you are now on your own with your Money Machine. You certainly look forward to that first incredible payout and sincerely hope the money continues for months, years, and decades to come.

Thank you for indulging me in my money machine story. We had a bit of fun with the narrative, but the money machine story is about real-life truth. Part of the magic of being ALIVE and WELL is the potential to create your own story and live your own life as an adult. Our childhoods are meant to shape us into the most capable adults possible so that we can make a difference in the world.

As you become an adult, you unlock the potential to work hard and earn a steady income every day, week, or month of your life. There isn't some dramatic festival that ushers you into adulthood (usually). Certainly, you won't stumble into a traveling shop that just gives you a literal money machine that spits out thousands of dollars for nothing.

Economically, you are the MONEY MACHINE. You have irreplaceable parts that function well (God willing) as long as you take care of yourself, work hard, and avoid certain breakdowns in life.

The unfortunate reality is that nobody's money machine is never-ending. Each of us certainly has an end to our ability to work hard and earn a living. Some are blessed with 90 years of life, working up until the day they die. I'm reminded of someone like Clint Eastwood, who put out a film when he was over 90 years old.[8] Others, like Michael J. Fox who was diagnosed with Parkinson's disease at only age 29,[9] get debilitating illnesses through no fault of their own. Like it or not, many of us will get hit by many unavoidable setbacks in life that can severely damage the one-of-a-kind money machines known as our Human Life Value. Let's once again quote Die Neatly:

> ***"There are only three things that can happen to you: you live, you die, or you become disabled. In Human Life Value terms, you either will reach your full potential (you live a long life), you lose it all (you die), or it's greatly diminished (you become disabled)."***[10]

Insuring Your Future

The reality of irreversible damage to your earnings potential is why it is critical to protect yourself with products like life insurance. The money machine concept is a way to help you think more clearly about the need for defensive financial planning. Seriously consider, if you had that literal money machine product with irreplaceable parts, wouldn't you want to insure it? We insure our cars, our houses, and more. If you have something that pays you thousands of dollars every month for decades, it would be irresponsible to not insure it if you could.

---

[8]   Clint Eastwood filmography. Wikipedia. https://en.wikipedia.org/wiki/Clint_Eastwood_filmography

[9]   Michael J. Fox. The Michael J. Fox Foundation. https://www.michaeljfox.org/bio/michael-j-fox

[10]   Die Neatly. Jim Lusk. 2020. Page 67

Your Human Life Value is your money machine. If you are worth $2,000,000 in HLV, then you want to make sure nothing destroys that value. The way you make sure is by insuring yourself. When I talk with people about life insurance, I like to tell them that I'm sure they are wonderful people who love their kids and their spouses. But, economically speaking, they are money machines: they go to work and bring home cash. But what if a bus hits them one day and that's all gone? That's the reality for all of us: we work hard but it could be gone tomorrow.

Therefore, the goal is to protect your future income with the right amount of protection. We can use the 4% rule to determine what is the right amount. The 4% rule is a measure of how much money you can safely withdraw every year without decreasing the original investment portfolio.[11] This assumes you prudently invest your money. For instance, if you have $1,000,000 in an investment account, 4% of that is $40,000 per year. If that account earns over 4% each year (which is a very reasonable rate of return), then you can withdraw 4% safely ($3,333 per month) and never go below $1,000,000 in that investment account. Therefore, life insurance, when done right, acts as a replacement money machine for you that works in perpetuity. This again assumes that you prudently invest the life insurance proceeds and only withdraw 4% per year or less.

Another Die Neatly quote: **"Once people realize their lives (in Human Life Value terms) are one-of-a-kind devices for achieving their financial dreams, they see the wisdom in insuring their own futures through life insurance."[12]**

Your Last Love Letter

Who are the most important people to you in the whole world? The answer for most is our significant other and children, if we have those relationships. When we're young and single, we may not think about

---

[11]   What is the 4% rule… ? https://www.bankrate.com/retirement/what-is-the-4-per-cent-rule/
[12]   Die Neatly. Jim Lusk. 2020. Page 77.

what would happen if we died too often. Once we get into a serious relationship and get married, we now have a responsibility to our spouse.

Especially once we have children, we hopefully realize life isn't just about us anymore. Most of us want to devote ourselves to our spouses and kids. We would do anything for them, so we think. What about if you die or get disabled? What are you willing to do to plan for your decline or death? If you don't take into account the reality that you could get hit by a bus tomorrow, you aren't taking care of your family as best you should be. Let me introduce another concept from Die Neatly: your last love letter.[13]

Speaking to the married people out there, do you remember when you were first dating your now spouse? Hopefully, you took him or her out to special places and nice restaurants. Somehow you got the person to marry you, probably through careful relationship development. The poetic ones out there may have even written love letters. You get bonus points for old-fashioned hand-written letters, instead of just "love texts" or messages.

You likely put your heart into your letters, wanting to express your devotion in written words. Well, as strange as it sounds, life insurance is a love letter. It is a written expression of your devotion to your family, promising to take care of them even if the unthinkable happens and you die too soon. It lets them live their best lives, even if you aren't there to celebrate life with them.

I bet you made vows and promises to your spouse, and I believe you've worked very hard to give your family a great life full of joy and grand adventures. I believe you'll make those dreams come true, to the best of your ability. There is the problem: **"No one has a lease on life. We're all one heartbeat from eternity. We just don't know which one. A momentary lapse on the highway, a body temperature change in 6 degrees either way, and we're not here. What's your plan?"** – Ben Feldman.

---

[13] See Die Neatly, Chapter 6: pages 80-85.

A Real Story of Tragedy and Love After Death

In my town, there was a man, not even 40 years old, who was one of the most devoted husbands. He also adored his children. He was a cheerful man, beloved by his family and coworkers. Then one summer day he went out with the family and an accident occurred. He was killed. It was a devastating tragedy, and it couldn't have happened to a nicer, more kind-hearted man. As you can imagine, his family grieved so deeply at this horrible loss.

Once reality set in, the family had to figure out how to live day by day, including managing all the mundane financial affairs. It was then, that his family discovered this man's last love letter: a life insurance policy that allowed his family to maintain their current lifestyle. I don't believe he ever got to say goodbye, dying so suddenly, but thank God he had the foresight to plan for his own untimely death. This truly was a final expression of love from beyond the grave to his precious wife and children.

The hard truth is that any of us could be in that man's position. No matter how fit, strong, and capable we are, or how compassionate and caring, a freak accident could take us out of this life. If we say we love our families, can we prove it based on our financial decisions? Do we have a life insurance portfolio that shows our full devotion?

There was another man who wanted to love his family, but he made bad financial decisions. They lived in a small house (you could call it a shack), and barely survived day by day. One day, this husband came home with a brand-new chainsaw, very proud of it, even though his family was struggling to pay for food. I also believe he had no life insurance. What if he took that new chainsaw to cut down a tree, and it fell on him and killed him? What would be the memory of his family without a final life insurance love letter?

You can have great tools and other worldly goods, but what happens if you also get cut down by disease or death? Will your family lose the house? Can you still send your kids to college in years to come? Will your spouse feel pressure to remarry out of financial need? When a spouse dies, the other may need to take care of the kids as a full-time endeavor.

Will there be enough money for the surviving spouse not to worry about working "outside of the home".?

I heard a pastor say that his working definition of love was simply "being committed to another person." I want to be committed to my family, even in the event of my death. Life insurance lets me provide even if some tragedy takes me away. I want my wife to know that she will be taken care of, either by me here on earth, or by the future benefits of my committed financial planning while I was still alive.

By the way, I hope you know you still can write love letters to your spouse. Many of us struggle to date, give gifts, and celebrate our spouses once we've been married for many years. Here's some free marriage advice: write a hand-written letter of love to your spouse. Do that and also build a strong life insurance portfolio (usually meaning multiple policies, tailored to your specific needs). Then talk to your spouse (and kids, if they are old enough) about your portfolio and the importance of planning for even the worst events. Let your spouse know you love them enough to plan for the worst. We can so easily be inconsiderate and not plan as well as many of our spouses would like. Getting life insurance (and setting up a will or trust) may help your spouse know he or she matters. This type of planning helps your whole family know you are thinking beyond yourself and about their security.

The Blessing of Life Insurance

A few people accrue enough money that they know their family will be okay if they were to die. Most of us aren't in that situation and don't have $5 million in the bank. Even if you do, a life insurance portfolio still makes sense since you can afford it (assuming you are in good health and can get insured). For us regular folks, the only way to ensure our family's lifestyle after our death is to have a way to replace our income upon our death.

Remember our money machine example? Death destroys our money machine and robs us of perhaps our greatest gift: time. You can always earn more money if you have the time (and health) to work. Like the beloved father who died just shy of 40 years old, he lost out on his most productive, highest-earning years. He was just in a position to put his first couple of decades of work to good use and move into higher positions in his company.

I love life insurance so much because it steps into the void of death and transmutes lost time to immediately available cash. It is unique because it is a financial contract that matures upon an event rather than over time. That terrible event, death, is just when a family needs some relief and a little bit of positive news. This is my joy as a life insurance professional: to help give families a sort of second wind when the unthinkable happens and threatens to wipe them out.

I also love life insurance because it's one of the few products that people buy almost exclusively for altruistic reasons. Think about it: very few people buy life insurance for selfish reasons. You buy it because you're serious about taking care of those who rely on you. Unlike the guy who bought a chainsaw and was likely only thinking of himself, buying life insurance shows you have a perspective beyond yourself and are willing to take real steps to plan for others. That is mature love.

Again, I know you love your family. Otherwise, you likely wouldn't read books like this. Life insurance is a love letter, but only you can choose to write it. Many people just think nice thoughts but don't take the next steps to speak and communicate their feelings to others. Don't just feel love for your family. Be moved to act, craft a beautiful and wise "last love letter" by working with an experienced life insurance agent and company to get the policy (ies) in force now. Your life is worth protecting, and your family deserves the assurance of your love even beyond your life on earth.

Peace of Mind: Priceless

By the way, one of the most unexpected benefits of life insurance is the "peace of mind" you get today. Oftentimes, people downplay life insurance because they think nothing bad will happen to them. Moreover, they think life insurance only gives some unlikely benefit decades down the road. Both mentalities are flawed. One of the most immediate benefits of life insurance is the incredible "peace of mind" you get when you finally sign the contract and get it done. Once you own life insurance, you know that your family WILL have money if you die. You know those Mastercard commercials that use the "priceless" tagline regarding the memories we make?[14] Well, the feeling of knowing your family will be okay, even if you die or get disabled really is priceless.

Life insurance is about ensuring life for your loved ones can continue better than it would have without it. If you die without protection, you most likely leave your family in a terrible financial position. There is a widow whose husband died of cancer almost 40 years ago. Her boys weren't even teenagers when he died, and his death forever changed their lives. However, the boys are now grown men living their lives.

Thankfully, before his death, the husband wrote his last love letter and made sure to have life insurance. So many years later, the widow is still being blessed by that life insurance money, receiving literal financial dividends month by month. She has had a wonderful peace of mind over so many years, knowing that money has been available to her. And what a wonderful tribute to her husband. He's been gone for so long, but the fruits of his financial love letter are still producing benefits for his wife. How wonderful is that? He is still providing for her, in a sense. Don't you want that legacy, too?

This is also why we call it life insurance instead of death insurance. We are in the business of helping people have life after tragedies. It is for the living. You pay premiums now to protect against a much worse situation down the road. Much like our talk of saving versus spending in the last chapter, there is a big peace of mind in sacrificing some money today in premiums for the benefit of life insurance saving the day when your family needs it most. This is why my prior book was called Die Neatly. We don't want to leave ugly messes after we're gone, if we can help it. Help your family today by writing your last love letter and providing peace of mind to you, your spouse, and your family today and down the road if the worst happens.

---

[14]   Mastercard. Marking 25 years of Priceless. https://www.mastercard.com/news/perspectives/2022/priceless-25-year-anniversary/

Life Insurance 101 (Adapted from Die Neatly)

This book can't possibly cover everything about actually getting life insurance, but here are some basics. There are two types of life insurance: term and permanent. Both have a place. Beware of people who make extreme statements like "only buy term life insurance." I call these people termites. I define termites as closed-minded financial planners who try to solve every life insurance problem with term policies. An open-minded advisor will see a purpose for both term and permanent policies. There is a reason why both term and permanent life insurance policies have existed for a long, long time: there is a time and place for both, based on your unique needs and situation.

The big difference between term and permanent is that term can be thought of as renting and permanent can be thought of as owning. Both renting and owning have their place and likely make sense for you based on the seasons of your life. With term life insurance, you 'rent' your life insurance each month and year by paying the premiums. You can decide to stop paying the premiums, which means you give up your term insurance, much like how you stop paying rent on an apartment and move elsewhere. Permanent life insurance, like buying a home, can be more costly at first, but comes with great benefits.

Perhaps you can already see that there is no one right answer to whether you should buy term or permanent life insurance. When clients ask me this question, I say, "It depends on how long you want life insurance." When you're young and hopefully healthy, buying a large amount of relatively inexpensive term life insurance makes sense. As you get older and start to earn more money, you can afford to buy (or convert some of your term life insurance into) permanent life insurance that you can keep until your death, even in old age. I call this an "inevitable payout" for an "inevitable gain."

Below are comparison lists between term and permanent and a visual diagram of the premium differences in dollars between the two, taken from Die Neatly.[15]

---

[15]   Die Neatly. Jim Lusk. Pages 90-91.

fe Insurance

Like renting—lower cost earlier in the policy, but gets really expensive after the "term"

- Increasing premium at some time, probably before you die (only 1-2% pays claims)

- No equity—no cash value

- Pays "if you die" during the term, greater than 98% don't

- Self-evicting: the company has designed the product to "evict you" before life expectancy

- Cheaper (lower cost) early then reality hits—it gets very (maybe too) expensive as you get older

- 20- and 30-year term is just "pre-funding" future mortality charges—like prepaying rent. That would be okay, but over 75% are lapsed or replaced within 10 years. So, you "prepaid" and may never receive a discount later.

- Death benefit only: (like most insurance policies, home, auto, etc.)...some have terminal illness or Long Term care accelerated death benefits.

Permanent Life Insurance

- Like owning—higher premium, but some goes into equity

- Level premium—can be guaranteed to never increase

- For life if funded properly, even beyond age 100

- Equity (called cash value) is accessible "tax-free" if set up properly

- Pays "when you die" (versus "if" with term insurance)

- Self-completing: you don't have to pay for life to get lifetime coverage

- More expensive earlier but level offset by cash value

- Inevitable Death benefit plus access to "living benefit" (cash value)—for "pennies on the dollar"

- Can provide accelerated money for long-term care, terminal illness, or other critical illnesses

DIAGRAM: Life Insurance – Term versus Permanent (Curved Line vs Flat Line)

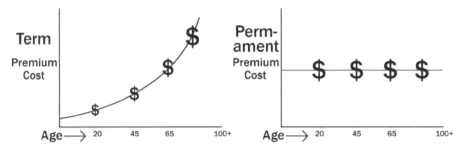

Whether you need term, permanent, or both, you want to talk with a qualified, certified expert. As much as I love life insurance, the world is full of dishonest salespeople who will try to get you to buy suspiciously cheap life insurance, either through the mail, some 1-800 number, or online. I call this bad term. Bad term life insurance is with a poorly rated company and isn't convertible. Good term life insurance is with a highly rated company and convertible, meaning you can turn it into (convert) to permanent life insurance down the road (within the term conversion period) without another health exam to requalify. Thus, convertible term life insurance is like a "lease with an option to buy" in the Real Estate world. That's why it's called Good Term vs Cheap Term (the bad term above). My mother used to say, "cheap things aren't good and good things aren't cheap". That's true with life insurance too.

There is so much more to be said about the precise details of getting life insurance. The goal is to build a custom-tailored life insurance portfolio that takes into account your specific needs, income, and situation. This portfolio should be updated as you go through various stages of life. There is no "one policy" to rule them all. Once we understand our human life value, we can begin quantifying our life insurance needs. Most of our clients have both term and permanent life insurance for a well-designed "portfolio". I hope your advisor takes that same approach.

Disability (Adapted from Die Neatly)

Before we end this chapter, one final section is needed to talk about disability. In my 2020 book, Die Neatly, I described disability as 'the living death.' I say this because disability can be a double-whammy of losing your ability to work and losing your ability to care for yourself. This means you might not be able to produce an income for your family, on top of that, your family may have to spend so much of their time and money taking care of you (feeding you, clothing you, rehabilitating you). You are alive, but your old productive life has probably diminished.

In terms of our Money Machine analogy, disability is when your Money Machine starts to sputter and break down yet isn't completed destroyed (death). No longer does your Money Machine produce money every month; rather the Money Machine requires you to insert money into it each month to stay operational. These costs represent the healthcare needs you will have when disabled.

If you, God forbid, become disabled, hopefully you have a loving family to take care of you. Ideally, they will be thankful you are alive and glad to take care of you. Still, if your spouse has to quit his or her job to care for you full-time, or your family has to hire full-time caretakers for you, these costs for care and lost income can bring your family to the breaking point financially (and emotionally).

The way you protect yourself and your family is to get disability income protection insurance. This simply means that your income will be replaced if you become disabled. To illustrate the value, consider the following two choices regarding purchasing disability income protection. You have the choice of Job A or Job B:

- ☐ Job A – $100,000/year, if disabled: income = $0

- ☐ Job B – $98,000/year, if disabled: income = $60,000/year

If you picked Job B, you just purchased a disability income insurance policy that costs $2,000 per year in premiums and provides $60,000 per year ($5,000 per month) if you become disabled. This is wise, important planning. You decide to have a 2% reduction in money for the 'peace of mind' of years and years of disability income protection. Guarding your Human Life Value is the most important insurance you will ever buy, and this insurance includes both life and disability insurance.

Disability insurance is important and necessary, especially if you have a high-paying "white collar" job like a doctor, dentist, attorney, or engineer where there's little chance of disability occurring but a huge financial loss if it happens. Professions like construction, plumbing, and landscaping have a higher probability of occurrence. Therefore, the premium is usually really high, and benefits can be limited, so it's likely not worth purchasing because it's too expensive relative to your income. Plus, some occupations simply can't be insured (coded as RNA, risk not available).

Even though disability insurance is so crucial, it can be the most confusing, misunderstood insurance you will ever purchase. I recommend a disability insurance specialist who can compare several companies and, depending on occupation class and desired coverage, find you the best deal. At the very least, make sure your advisor is experienced in disability income protection.

Personally, I don't believe in paying extra premiums for short-term disability because once the short term runs out, if you're still disabled, the income still is gone, and those premiums can be better allocated toward the savings needed for emergencies. Insurance should only be to cover those catastrophic losses: medical expenses, premature death, disability income protection, long-term care expenses, and home/auto/liability insurance. I cannot recommend expensive maintenance insurance, short-term disability, or accident/cancer policies. Put that money into an HSA or FSA account (pre-tax money) to pay the deductible on your medical insurance. Again, get a qualified advisor involved here.

Chapter Conclusion

After reading this chapter, you can see why both premature death and disability are essential to plan for, despite how unpleasant those events are to consider. You are many things, but financially you are a one-of-a-kind Money Machine. If you get damaged or break down, you (and your family) could be devastated financially. This is why we get life insurance and disability income insurance. While we want to live and plan and grow as if we're going to be alive for countless decades, there is great peace of mind knowing that you have prepared for premature death or disability.

There are only three things that can happen to this Money Machine (you): You live a long time, you die prematurely, or you become disabled. Please plan for all three scenarios!

Part 2

Social Security Retirement

2-A: Introducing Social Security Retirement

In Part 1, we gave you the good news that you likely are worth millions of dollars in human life value. The more you hone yourself and work hard, the more you can close the gap between your potential financial success and your actual bank account balances. Now, in Part 2, we further expand your worth by introducing another living money machine: Social Security retirement.

A Government Money Machine

In America, everyone who has earned income also pays into the Federal government's Social Security program. Such contributions are mandatory if you have W-2 income. Some don't realize it, but every paycheck you've received as an employee has had 7.65% (and your employer also pays 7.65%, totaling 15.3%[16]) of your hard-earned money removed and sent off to the Federal government. Even if you are self-employed, when it comes time to pay your taxes, Uncle Sam grabs a chunk of your money as self-employment tax. If you own your own business, you pay both sides of the payroll tax (15.3% of your Adjusted Gross Income). This Tax Is 6.2% for Social Security and 1.45% for Medicare. The total of these two is called FICA (Federal Insurance Contributions Act). We will just be focusing on Social Security.

In return for this significant tax on your labor, you get what we could call a mandated living money machine. It is mandated because the Federal

---

[16]   The government charges 6.2% to the employee and another 6.2% to the employer. Then there is also a 1.45% Medicare portion paid by both the employee and employer. These four percents add up to the real 15.3% tax that could have gone to you instead of the government. See https://www.ssa.gov/pubs/EN-05-10022.pdf

government requires nearly everyone to participate in the system. living because it pays you a lifetime income if you qualify. To qual you must work and report wages to the Social Security Administratic (SSA) for at least 40 quarters (cumulatively 10 years). Once you qualify and your benefit is calculated (based on your highest 35 of 40 years of reported wages), you can draw your Social Security once you either become disabled (per the SSA's rules) or reach early retirement age (age 62 for most[17] age 60 for widows and widowers)

Social Security's disability benefit is too complex to discuss in this book.[18] Rather, we will focus exclusively on the retirement portion of Social Security since it is an important part of nearly every American's retirement. For instance, statistics show that the monthly Social Security check at full retirement age (67 currently) is about $1,800.[19] Data also shows that these benefits account for an average of 25.40% of most people's retirement income.[20] In addition, Social Security benefits are estimated to replace about 42% of what an average income earner made before retirement. Therefore, Social Security retirement is a big deal, yet very few carefully study this future mandated income as they go through their working years.

To recap, Social Security retirement gives you a lifetime income at retirement, as long as you qualified for it by paying into Social Security for 10 years (40 quarters). This period can be consecutive or not; it doesn't matter. Once you qualify, your actual benefit is determined by the highest 35 of 40 years of earnings, compared to the wage base each year which the Social Security Administration determines this social security wage base for every calendar year. It is adjusted for inflation and currently is $168,600 for the year 2024. This means you would need to

---

[17]   Social Security Age Reduction. https://www.ssa.gov/benefits/retirement/planner/agereduction.html

[18]   A disability applicant must go through the SSA's complicated Disability Determination Process, which is beyond the scope of this book.

[19]   Social Security 2023: What's the Average Benefit at Every Age? Yahoo! Finance. Retrieved Sept. 15, 2023. https://finance.yahoo.com/news/average-social-security-benefit-every-120016509.html

[20]   Source needed for 25.40% number.

0 in wages for the tax year 2024 to ensure you maximize rement benefit for that year (1 out of 35 tested).

ial Security Controversies

ile social security retirement may seem like a bland topic, there two hotly contested issues surrounding it. The first issue is how much you should pay into Social Security. Remember that you pay social security taxes on your W-2 income or your Adjusted Gross Income for self-employed individuals. The Social Security Administration sets a maximum wage base each year (that goes up yearly based on inflation). Going over that amount will not increase your eventual social security retirement benefits. But being below that cap ($168,600 in 2024), will mean lower benefits down the road when you retire.

So, should you try to increase your W-2 income or Adjusted Gross Income to reach the wage base cap each year? This question isn't relevant to people who simply struggle to earn a modest living and earn around the median yearly individual income of around $55,000.[21] Moreover, most people aren't able to set their own W-2 wages or increase or decrease their Adjusted Gross Income. However, those who own their own businesses and pay wages to themselves may very well wrestle with the question of whether to hit the social security wage base.

In addition, what about married couples who both have decent incomes? If one or both are self-employed, should both people pay into social security? These questions of how much to pay into social security are the collective topic of the next chapter, Chapter 2-B, and I'll explain why you want to try to maximize your social security wages, if possible.

The even greater controversy revolves around when you should begin taking social security retirement since you can choose from early retirement age (62 for most), normal retirement age (NRA is 67 for most) or wait beyond that (up to age 70). I'll give you my simple answer: take your social security retirement benefits as soon as you can (unless

---

21 How Much Does the Average American Make in 2022? First Republic. December 7, 2022. https://www.firstrepublic.com/insights-education/how-much-does-the-average-american-make

you must take a reduced benefit between age 62 and NRA because you have too much earned income[22]). Explaining why I want Uncle Sam to show me my social security retirement money as soon as possible is the topic of Chapter 2-C.

To review, my position on Social Security retirement is twofold: maximize wages and draw immediately. The next two chapters will justify why I hold these positions, even while I acknowledge that what to pay in and when to draw are not only controversial but complex issues. After finishing Part 2, I believe you will be equipped with the necessary information to make the best Social Security retirement decisions for your life. We are talking about potentially hundreds of thousands (and even well over a million or two) of dollars in government mandated income. You don't want to wait until you're drawing social security to understand these concepts, so study while you're young if you can and reap the most rewards. Continue reading to learn how to maximize your Social Security retirement. This Money Machine for life is worth studying and maximizing.

---

[22] Receiving Benefits While Working. Social Security Administration. https://www.ssa.gov/benefits/retirement/planner/whileworking.html

2-B: Social Security: How to Maximize It

How much you get in Social Security retirement is determined by how high your wages were in relation to the annual social security wage base for your working years. Recall that social security uses the highest 35 of 40 years of earnings. If you have less than max "average indexed monthly earnings" (AIME) your benefits will be lower than if you had all those years accounted for.

Calculating the exact amount, you will receive isn't possible since we don't know what the future wage base numbers are, but, again, your benefit is based on your AIME. When it is time to collect benefits, the Social Security Administration adjusts (indexes) your past yearly wage data to compute an "average indexed monthly earnings" factor to get a "today's dollars" comparison for your highest 35 years earnings average (since a dollar was worth more in past years).

The actual benefit calculations are complicated.[23] Thankfully, we don't need to know all the rules. The most important thing to understand is that each year you want to get as close as possible to, or over the wage base limit if you want to maximize your social security retirement benefits. In short, know the wage base and try to increase your earnings up to that wage base dollar amount each year.

As noted in the prior chapter, many people, especially younger ones, will struggle to reach the current 2024 $168,600 wage base. If you're someone who works one job and receives a W-2 from your employer each year, you don't have much flexibility to adjust your earnings apart from trying to get promoted, receive a raise, or get a big bonus. You

---

[23]   Social Security Benefit Amounts. https://www.ssa.gov/OACT/COLA/Benefits.html

simply must try to make more W-2 income year after year increasing your AIME. By maxing out the contributions (matching the yearly wage base) for 35 years, you will receive the maximum benefit possible.

This is where Part 1 of this book comes into play again. Remember how we spoke of increasing your Human Life Value by furthering your education, skills, and training? When you increase your income through a side job, new business, or a strategic change of employers, you are not only increasing your Human Life Value but also your future social security retirement income.

Allow this synergistic effect to motivate you. If you work extra hard to further your own abilities and income in your early years, you will not only make more money to live better in the present, but you'll have more resources to save for your future and receive more in social security retirement.

Make a Game of It

I told you in Part 1 that I love to make games of things to take something dull and find a way to inject some fun. We noted you can track new skills you've learned, or raises you've received and give yourself rewards for 'winning' at your life goals each year. We can create a new game for social security retirement. But first, a caveat.

When I say 'game' I don't mean the ill-advised tricky financial games many people play. I played a lot of risky financial games over my life trying to guess the market. I would attempt to "buy low and sell high" in Real Estate, stocks, etcetera. I probably performed below average. The most successful financial decisions that I've made had to do with social security and buying "after-tax" accumulation tools like cash value life insurance and Roth IRAs. I also greatly benefited from furthering my education and credentials, which increased my human life value, as discussed in Part 1.

One thing I've certainly realized over my 40-plus years studying and planning for social security is this simple fact: **"If you want the maximum social security retirement, you have to maximize**

your contributions (up to the social security wage base) for 35 out of 40 years."

This may seem obvious, but many of my clients played the wrong game for 20-30 years by trying to minimize their personal business wages to save on taxes in the short term. Then, upon realizing their mistake, they tried to do a "Hail Mary" the last 10 years before retirement to catch up by maximizing their wages those limited years. This is not like the stock market where you can hit it big in a few years. Social Security has limits and conditions that play out over multiple decades of earnings. Thus, our Social Security retirement 'game' needs to be played over many years based on smart planning.

First, we look at the wage base each year. Go back to the year 2022. The wage base was $147,000. How close did you get to that wage? Get your tax return out if you need to and find your reported wages (and self-employment earnings subject to self-employment tax if you own a business). Maybe you made about half the wages, earning a nice $70,000 in 2022. Earning half the wage base doesn't mean your eventual benefits will be half of the maximum. They will be higher than this because there is a minimum benefit level that is higher than zero. Hence, there isn't a linear percentage calculation we can use to simply say, "You'll get 50% of your maximum benefit if you make 50% of the wage base for 35+ years."

Exact numbers aren't the goal. Rather, I want you to think of this game as taking 35 annual exams. Each one has a grade, and the grade is based on how close you got to the social security wage base for your salary that year. We looked at the year 2022. What about the year 2023? The wage base was $160,200. That jumped quite a bit from 2022. Many of us couldn't get a $13k+ raise to keep up with the wage base increase. Still, if you made $100,000, you were at about 62% of the max. That's like a grade of "D." Next year, can you get into the "C" range at over 70%? What about the "B" range of over 80%?

After 35 years, what's your grade point average? Achieving a "B" average means breaking 80% of the wage base. An "A" would mean you got very close to maxing out the wage base every year. Remember, Social Security takes the average of your highest 35 years of income relative to the wage base for that year. Even paying yourself $120,000 in 2023 earns you an "A" instead of an "A+" because you're $10,200 less than the wage base. See the table below.

Year	Wage Base	Salary	Percent	Grade
2015	$118,500	$120,000	101%	A+
2016	$118,500	$120,000	101%	A+
2017	$127,200	$120,000	94%	A
2018	$128,400	$120,000	93%	A
2019	$132,900	$120,000	90%	A-
2020	$137,700	$120,000	87%	B+
2021	$142,800	$120,000	84%	B
2022	$147,000	$120,000	82%	B-
2023	$160,200	$120,000	75%	C
2024	$168,400	$120,000	71%	C-

We use this "wage grade" game to help motivate you to maximize this aspect of your living money machine. If you get straight A's, you are setting yourself up for a great baseline "wake-up" money from Social Security at retirement. To best play the game, know the rules, which is what this book teaches (35 highest years relative to the Social Security wage base). As we noted, if you work at a typical W-2 job for an employer, do the obvious (work hard, try for raises, and ask for bonuses). Also try to switch to different companies if the opportunity is better. Make yourself valuable in the market through education, a strong track record of performance, and networking.

To really "play the game," you must be able to set your own wages, which usually only self-employed people can do (like in a privately held Corporation or LLC). The next sections of this chapter will transition to strategies for self-employed people. Even if you aren't self-employed presently, let the rest of this chapter motivate you to consider branching out and starting a business or such.

If you happen to be in the fortunate self-employed position, the goal is to set your wage as close to the Social Security wage base as possible. You want to achieve an "A+" in life, right? Why not shoot for an "A+" in

Social Security retirement, too? Remember, to get an A+, you just need to match the Social Security wage base. If you earn over that wage base, the good news is that the W-2 income above the Social Security wage base is only taxed at 1.45% vs 7.65% (2.9% vs 15.3% for self-employed over the wage base.

My Personal Story

Allow me to use my personal story again to explain going from W-2 wages to setting your own. When I was much younger, working at my high school teaching job, I naturally got a monthly paycheck and a W-2 at the end of the year. I earned what the state set as wages for my government teaching position. Then when I first started my practice in the financial services business, I became a "statutory W-2" employee. That meant the company paid half of the Social Security, but I still got to use a Schedule C for business expenses. A statutory W-2 employee is sort of like a halfway point between being a confined W-2 employee and being my own boss as an independent contractor.

As far as my first financial industry pay, I was making over $60,000 per year in the early 1980s. My income increased rapidly, and I realized after a few years that I could control my expenses to determine my Adjusted Gross Income (AGI) on my tax return. This was the luxury of running my own business. If I could set my AGI over the Social Security wage base, I would be getting an A+ grade each year. That realization meant 'game on'!

Thus, one of my yearly goals was to always hit the Social Security wage base (see table) every year as early as possible in the calendar year so that for the balance of the year the IRS would only require me to withhold 1.45% versus 7.65% (the other 6.2% is only charged up to the SS wage base). Some years, I would hit that number in the first quarter, and I made sure I always knew when I maxed out the wage base. In fact, for 22 years from 1995 to 2017, I was a W-2 employee in upper management with a Fortune 100 financial services company and was fortunate to get "A+" grades early each year.

Plan, Track, & Verify

My plan to hit the wage base worked well because my income was outpacing the increases in the wage base each year. It's much more difficult for those of you 15-20 years from retirement because the Social Security Administration have been making much larger increases to the wage base than back in the prior decades. We already noted that the year 2023's wage base jumped over $13,000 compared to 2022's (almost a 9% increase). Here is a short table of the history of the social security wage base.

Year	Wage Base
2024	$168,600
2023	$160,200
2020	$137,700
2015	$118,500
2010	$106,800
2005	$90,000
2000	$76,200
1995	$61,200
1990	$51,300
1985	$39,600
1980	$25,900

As an aside, notice the massive difference between the wage base over about 40 years. In 1980, you only had to make about $26k to hit the wage base. In 2020, you needed nearly $140k. That means the wage base is about 5.4 times higher after 40 years (that's a 4.3% compounded growth, larger than normal pay raises). This really puts the power of inflation (for good and bad) into perspective. More practically, inflation hits those hardest who don't continue to grow their skills, adapt, and find new ways to make more money. This helps explain why it gets harder and harder to keep up with the cost of living each year, including achieving good Social Security retirement grades!

Speaking of, how has your income been relative to the wage base when you look over the decades, if you've been working that long? Please keep your score. If not this "wage grade" game, find another game or personal reward system (I'll buy X for myself or my family if I hit Y wages this year). Thinking positively will help you feel better about the big chunk of Social Security taxes (6.2% on your side, another 6.2% from your employer, if you have one) coming out of each paycheck.

Back when I first played this 'wage grade' game, the internet wasn't even available to most people. If you wanted to track what social security listed as your wages each year, it was much more difficult. Nowadays, we have the big luxury of a good social security website that displays your wages over the years. Go to SSA.gov and set up your My SSA account. They will have a record of your earnings. See how accurate they are. Verify your wages each year because the SSA can make (and has made) mistakes. So, "audit your grade." Do not just trust the government to get it right. If there is a mistake, go through the process to get your reported wages corrected with the Social Security Administration.

Self-Employed Wages

Now that you know the benefits of playing the Social Security retirement wage base 'game,' let's dive deep into methods to maximize your wage base as an entrepreneur. Self-employed people have many choices on how to run their businesses. One big decision is about how much to pay yourself. Many self-employed people are led down the wrong path toward immediate gratification rather than "deferred gratification." What I'm referring to is an example of an S-Corp or LLC that chooses a very low salary and then the balance of the profit "is not subject to payroll taxation" (Social Security). So, the business is saving 15.3% on the portion of the profit that wasn't W-2 wage income. This short-term tax savings is very appealing, but there are two big problems with it.

First, it may be wrong, both ethically and accounting-wise. If you are purposefully paying yourself a salary far below the market rate for your skills and experience, the IRS won't be happy. They are auditing many businesses that pay such low salaries, suggesting that the compensation is "unreasonable" and too low for what work is being done by the recipient(s).

Second, paying yourself such a low wage can have the long-run effect of lowering your earnings record with the Social Security Administration. In our "game terms," paying yourself an artificially low salary means getting bad wage base grades and suffering lower social security retirement benefits down the road.

Let's consider an example scenario. You own a single-owner S-Corp (or LLC) with a gross revenue of $2,000,000 a year. Your expenses and cost of goods and services total about $1,000,000. Thus, you are doing very well with a yearly net profit of about $1,000,000. What should your wage be? Many in this scenario opt for a very low wage for themselves, wanting to avoid paying FICA.

Say a buddy of yours tells you to pay yourself $50,000. Maybe you even find an accountant that encourages such a low salary. This means only $50,000 would be subject to Social Security and Medicare taxes (7.65% total) and State/Federal payroll taxes. The other $950,000 profit is subject only to State and/or Federal income taxes. The IRS sees this 'low wage but high profit' position as manipulating the system when you really made closer to a million dollars. This can really agitate the IRS and encourage them to inspect your whole business much more closely and conduct an expensive audit. One time an IRS agent audited a business and suspected a business owner of unscrupulous behavior and began denying many expenses. This agent even reclassified a $50 'Happy Birthday' check as business income because they didn't trust the taxpayer.

Even if you can afford to spend thousands of dollars going to IRS tax court to fight back, the IRS can cause serious misery to you if they believe you're the type that is trying to evade taxes. I suppose the lesson is this: if you're unreasonable, the IRS may be unreasonable right back at you. Moreover, a meager $50,000 wage would give you a failing wage base grade, given the current $168k+ social security wage base. To avoid a failing grade and possible serious IRS problems, what "reasonable compensation" is appropriate?

What if you paid yourself a large $500,000 wage and still got the other $500,000 profit? This likely would avoid IRS problems. It also would give you well beyond an A+ wage base grade. In fact, once you hit the current wage base ($168,400 in 2024), everything from that point up to $500,000 is only taxed at the Medicare 1.45% rate instead of the combined 7.65% rate. If you count the business half of the tax, the total would be 2.9% versus 15.3%.

However, unless you're a self-employed doctor or something like that, $500,000 as a wage is likely excessive. A compromise in this case would be setting your wage at $180-200k. This is much more reasonable than the initial $50,000 wage, and you would still max out your social security earnings for the year by making more than the wage base. In addition, you still have a very profitable business.

Sole Proprietors versus Corporations

To clarify, setting your own wage is something you can usually only do if you have an incorporated business. Sole proprietors don't have this luxury since they don't take a wage but rather a draw against the "bottom-line" at the end of the tax year. Therefore, a sole proprietor that has a profit over the social security wage base amount will still max out his or her social security wage for the year (such as in the prior $1,000,000 profit example above).

Unfortunately, that sole proprietor will also pay the 2.9% Medicare tax on his or her entire profit. The corporation gets the benefit of only paying the 2.9% Medicare tax on the wages paid. To see the tax savings difference, consider the following comparison using a $200,000 salary (called a draw for the sole proprietor).

	Sole Proprietor		S-Corp or LLC	
Gross Revenue	$2,000,000		$2,000,000	
Expenses	$1,000,000		$1,000,000	
Draw/Salary	$200,000		$200,000	
Profit	$800,000	(all subject to payroll taxes)	$800,000	(not subject to payroll taxes)
SS 12.4%	$19,865	(up to wage base)	$19,865	(up to wage base)
Medicare 2.9%	$29,000	(on entire profit)	$5,800	(only on $200k)
Additional tax cost	**$23,200**		--	You save a ton!

Some people say it's too expensive or cumbersome to set up an LLC or S-Corp. However, notice you are saving $23,200 in the example above for just one year. For that chunk of change, you can afford the time and benefits of changing the structure of your business. You also get other advantages like limiting your liability. On the other hand, I've had many acquaintances and friends who started businesses and barely made enough to support their families and thus paid little or nothing into Social Security and bragged about it...then they complain about their small retirements. Why?

Still, if you're a sole proprietor with a significant yearly profit, please consult a qualified CPA or good tax attorney to help you navigate structuring your business entity and wages. Also have whoever you work with help you decide how much W-2 wages are reasonable and tell them about your social security "wage game" aiming to max out the wage base each year.

In contrast, I had friends who worked in construction-related businesses their whole lives and were independent contractors (either Sole Proprietors, LLCs, or Corporations). They did very well for themselves but didn't report all their earnings. They, instead, opted for 'under the table' cash transactions to avoid taxes.

They also exaggerated (or fabricated) expenses on their tax returns to greatly reduce their taxable income. They would reduce their AGI (Adjusted Gross Income), sometimes even to zero. Then they would brag, over a drink, how little taxes they paid, while they lived an abundant lifestyle with new trucks, boats, ATVs, etcetera. Well, now they're paying dearly for their "immediate gratification" and poor choices because they have very little retirement savings. All those years of not paying into Social Security retirement means and their monthly benefit is toward the minimum amount ($1,033 in 2024 with 30 years of contributions) vs approaching the maximum ($3,822 in $2024). That range over 25 years of drawing benefits with COLAs could be over $1,000,000. We may be created equally, but our Social Security benefits are far from equal. Please get as close each year to the SS Wage Base as you can.

Likewise, some don't even file tax returns and operate entirely on cash. This is very dangerous. I knew of an extremely talented builder/carpenter who did this. His woodworking skills were exquisite, but his financial judgment was so rough that he hadn't filed taxes for over 10 years. He didn't think the IRS would ever catch up to him, and he was happy living an "off the grid" cash-only life. I don't know what happened to him, but I can certainly tell you that his many years of not reporting income meant that he was cutting himself off from enjoying Social Security retirement one day. Remember, you need 40 quarter credits (10 years) to even be eligible for Social Security benefits at retirement. So, at least get in "the game" by accumulating 40 quarter credits. Unreported cash transactions won't help you qualify. Doing everything "under the table" means no social security credits earned and no retirement benefits later! Don't cheat in "the game!"

As already noted, the goal is not to see how low you can get your Social Security taxes to be. The goal is to run a growing business with increasing income and benefits for your family. Running a business is hard. It's especially tough to be profitable and sustainable. My recommendation is to spend more time and money on marketing to grow your business, keep your expenses under control, pay your fair share of taxes (including social security), and plan for your succession. Seek mentors, coaches, and talent who can help you. And remember, be "reasonable" so that others (including the IRS) will be "reasonable" back to you.

Another Example: $500k Income

Below is another mathematical table for a business owner making $500,000 per year (salary plus profit) who can set his or her own salary. With the same expenses, the extra income would be profit and only taxed at Federal (and State, if applicable) income tax rates and not subject to Social Security taxes.

Salary	Profit	Total Income	Social Security Tax (12.4%)	Medicare Tax (2.9%)	FICA Tax Total (15.3%)
$50,000	$450,000	$500,000	$6,200	$1,450	$7,650
$100,000	$400,000	$500,000	$12,400	$2,900	$15,300
$150,000	$350,000	$500,000	$18,600	$4,350	$22,950
* $168,600	$331,400	$500,000	$20,906	$4,889	$25,796
/* $200,000	$300,000	$500,000	$20,906	$5,800	$26,706
/* $300,000	$200,000	$500,000	$20,906	$8,700	$29,606

*$168,600 is the 2024 Social Security wage base max.
**Not recommended since this wage is above the Social Security wage base max.
***This chart does not include the additional 0.9% Medicare tax for high-income earners.

If you show this to your CPA or business manager, they might think that you're crazy to choose to pay more social security tax. But look at the numbers. Remember, also that the IRS wants you to have "reasonable compensation." If you're only showing $50,000 as a successful entrepreneur, they may audit you and challenge your income (and you won't have any good defense). On the other hand, few occupations need to go over the social security wage base for income to remain "reasonable."

So, in the above example, should you declare a $100,000 salary or $168,600? The difference in social security tax that you control is $10,496 ($25,796 minus $15,300). Let's take a good look at what else you can do with that roughly $10k if you don't put it into social security tax. We will assume you've got 20 years until full retirement age, meaning you're age 47 and will draw social security retirement at age 67.

You could invest the $10,496 tax savings at a conservative 6% for 20 years and get a pretax value of $386,102. Using the 4% rule, that would pay out $15,444 per year at retirement indefinitely ($1,283 per month). Your reduced social security retirement will be at least that amount and have less of a cost-of-living adjustment (COLA).

At first blush, you could say, "I can do better than 6%, and I get to control it." Here is **what really happens** for most people.

1. You don't invest the difference; you consume it.

2. You don't get 6% year-in-and-year-out unless you take undue risk.

3. You forget to factor in the post-retirement COLA for social security retirement.

4. You listen to bad advice from people who are cheating the system and hurting themselves.

Point One. The nice thing about Social Security retirement is that is mandatory. If you pay into the system, you get a benefit. If you choose not to, you can easily prioritize spending today at the cost of tomorrow's savings. Plus, if you "cheat" and don't report wages you will probably get caught. Even if you don't, you know it's morally wrong and I believe that you won't be blessed.

Point Two. If you invest the difference, you have to carefully manage your investments. Many give in to the temptation of risky investments. Social security isn't flashy, but it is guaranteed.

Point Three. When you draw Social Security retirement, past earnings are indexed for current dollars. Then you also get a cost-of-living adjustment each year (only a few years equals zero). You don't get these benefits with other accounts such as many traditional pensions that cap their COLAs at 2-3%.

Point Four. We've already covered the dangers of bad advice. It is very risky to "minimize" your taxes, including social security taxes. It is also unethical and can be illegal. It is better to "give to Caesar what is his" and increase your reported income up to the social security wage base to ensure higher Social Security retirement income.

Point Five. Remember that this is a Money Machine for Life. The biggest fear for retirees in America is "outliving their money". This benefit is for your life...you can't outlive it!

What About Your Spouse?

You know I strongly believe in trying to maximize your Social Security, but this assumes you are the primary wage-earner in your life. If you're single, then you certainly want to maximize your wage base, each year, if possible. What about if you are married? This gets tricky since there are so many scenarios, such as two-income households split 50/50, one income earner while the other spouse tends the household, and everything in between these two situations.

As you probably already know, your spouse can either draw their own Social Security or half of yours (if you are married for one year or longer). Once at retirement, if your working-years incomes were close to each other, you would get the most money by each of you using your own social security records to draw from. This also depends on if one or both spouses choose to continue working and make over a certain income level ($22,320 per year in 2024). See the next chapter, Chapter 2-C, on when to draw.

If one spouse worked the entire marriage and the other took care of the home, then the homemaker spouse might not even qualify for Social Security retirement (if they didn't have 40 quarters of reported wages). In this situation, the answer is obvious: both spouses must draw from the working spouse's record. Again, the working spouse would get 100% of his or her benefit amount. The homemaking spouse would get 50% of that benefit (subject to early reduction prior to normal retirement age).

In today's world, it is often common for both spouses to work to some degree, but usually one spouse has the larger income. Perhaps a husband works at a factory full-time, but the wife also does part-time work when not taking care of the kids. Or a husband might be the one to stay home with the kids. Even though his wife works full-time, he also operates a part-time online business.

In either of the cases above, if you or your spouse have significantly different incomes (relative to the social security wage base), it may be in your best interest to plan on maximizing ONLY ONE of your social security incomes. This is especially true if both spouses operate their own businesses and have the flexibility of setting wages for themselves, as we discussed already in this chapter.

Choosing to maximize just one Social Security wage record means you would plan to have both spouses draw from that single record. In other words, the spouse with the much lower income would draw from the other spouse's income record at retirement.

Like many things in life, what is best can be determined with math.

Two Average Social Security Incomes (at normal retirement age)		
Wage Earner 1	Wage Earner 2	Total
$2,000/month	+ $2,000/month	+ $4,000/month
One Larger Income with Spousal Benefit (50%)		
Wage Earner 1	Wage Earner 2	
$3,500/month	+ $1,750/month	+ $5,250/month
		$1,250/month more

What about your specific situation? The Social Security Administration provides an online calculator to estimate your Social Security retirement benefit.[24] This can be accessed through your 'My Social Security' online account at www.ssa.gov/myaccount. If you're middle-aged and both you and your spouse have been working on and off over the years, visit that website and use the calculators to determine if you should start trying to maximize one of the accounts. Again, if you and your spouse both work traditional W-2 jobs and make a typical American salary of $60,000 to $100,000, you won't have much room to control what you pay into social security, unless you work at a second business. Still, it is good to understand whether you are going to both draw your own social security or use one single (highest earning) wage record. Let's look at an example.

An Example: Dual Social Security Contributors

Suppose a married couple owns a dentist practice that is an LLC. Spouse A is the dentist, and Spouse B is the business manager. Let's say the practice brings in the same $500,000 in income that we used in a prior example in this chapter. With $500,000 in income, the accountant

---

[24] Online Benefits Calculator. SSA website. https://www.ssa.gov/benefits/retirement/planner/AnypiaApplet.html

recommends establishing a yearly W-2 wage of $150,000 and $75,000, respectively, which means both spouses will pay into social security. Spouse A's $150,000 is close to the wage base, so he would get a B+ grade. Spouse B's $75,000 is less than half of the wage base, so she would get a failing grade in our wage base game. This grade situation is why I would challenge the accountant's recommendation. Let's look at the math, with the accountant's plan on top and my alternate plan on bottom.

Accountant's Plan

Spouse A Dentist	Spouse B Manager	Total Wages		Leftover Profit		Total Income	Soc. Sec. Tax	Spouse A Grade	Spouse B Grade
$150,000	$75,000	$225,000	+	$275,000	=	$500,000	$34,425	B+	F

My Alternate Plan

Spouse A Dentist	Spouse B Manager	Total Wages		Leftover Profit		Total Income	Soc. Sec. Tax	Spouse A Grade	Spouse B Grade
$165,000	$0	$165,000	+	$335,000	=	$500,000	$25,245	A+	F*
							($9,180 less)		

*Spouse B's grade is an F, but he or she will get 50% of Spouse A's retirement benefit.

This is so important. As a business owner, don't put your spouse on social security until you maximize yours. If your spouse never pays into the social security system, he or she is still eligible for the "spousal benefit." And if you're married for 10 years or longer, this spousal benefit is "vested." This means your spouse can even claim your benefit if they are single (either through death or divorce) when they apply for Social Security retirement benefits. This is a good thing for long marriages that end up in divorce.

Again, this is NOT theory. My wife, Debbie, was my personal assistant (and the best I ever hired) from 1989-1993. She did everything! My goal, like an attorney or doctor, was to maximize my "billable hours" by being in front of the most people. You have to have a great assistant in the financial services business if you want to spend most of your time meeting new clients and helping existing ones.

One time when I was speaking with our accountant, this person wondered how much I was going to pay my wife as my assistant. I said, "nothing."

Had I paid her a salary just to "pay her social security," I would have fallen out of my straight "As" goal for myself. And for what? Less Social Security retirement for both my wife and me at retirement.

Then again, this 'no pay to your spouse' strategy may be at odds with our prior discussion of "reasonable compensation." You can get into trouble with the IRS and some state agencies if you don't correctly set up your business and bookkeeping. Some may also find it problematic to not pay your spouse for work they perform, especially if you have a rocky relationship and eventually divorce.[25] Consult professional advice before making complex legal decisions on your own.

Thankfully, my wife was okay with no "official pay" during those 1989-1993 years, and I certainly gave her plenty of monthly spending money to use as she desired. Even if it would have been nice to brag about her large salary as my assistant, she was building up something much better than "bragging rights". She now gets half of my maximum Social Security monthly benefit (almost $1,700). This is despite her never reaching the required 40 quarters to be eligible for own social security benefits during all her years raising our kids and working on and off.

Please study this strategy if you have a family-owned business in which you can control the income. Even if you haven't formed a legal entity for your business like an LLC or Corporation, there are ways to set your self-employment income for husband-and-wife sole proprietors. When you file your taxes, you normally file a Schedule C and Schedule SE for self-employment taxes. These forms are linked to a single tax ID (Social Security number) for you or your spouse. You can choose to split your income between two Schedule Cs. If you do this, you will have one for you and one for your spouse. Then you also will have a Schedule SE for each of you, each linked to the corresponding Schedule C. Seek a professional CPA here.

No matter the legal structure of your business, there is always the challenge of fairly reporting who does what between a husband and wife in business together, but you want to make informed decisions based on

25   Can a Spouse Work for an LLC for No Pay? https://smallbusiness.chron.com/can-spouse-work-llc-pay-77333.html

accurate knowledge. Unfortunately, few advisors have studied this topic. Remember, one A+ Social Security income plus a "non-W-2" spouse will receive more in Social Security retirement benefits than two spouses each with "C" incomes.

Social Security Survivor Incomes

Now that we've looked at maximizing your Social Security earnings, we must also factor in what happens if a spouse dies. This planning is also affected by when the spouse dies, either in the middle of his or her working years or close to retirement.

The death of a spouse means the living spouse can claim the deceased spouse's Social Security benefit at retirement, assuming the surviving spouse is vested. Like the spousal benefit, the "widow(er)s" benefit is vested if the surviving spouse had been married to the deceased spouse for 10 years or longer and is presently not married to someone else. If the living spouse also qualifies for Social Security personally, he or she gets the largest of the two claims (but not both).

Consider this simple example starting with two living spouses at retirement. The retiree receives $3,500 per month. The spouse's earnings record is much lower than the retiree, so the spouse gets the 50% spousal benefit of $1,750 per month. The total is $5,250. See this simple chart summary:

	Retiree		Spousal		Total
Monthly	$3,500	+	$1,750	=	$5,250

But what if the retiree dies? Then the spouse can switch to the deceased spouse's record and receive $3,500 without the 50% spousal reduction. That is great for the spouse, but what isn't great at all is that the spouse still gets hit with an overall monthly benefit reduction of 33%. The math is: $5,250 - $3,500 = $1,750 | $1,750 / $5,250 = 33%. See this simple chart:

Both Spouses	Deceased Spouse	Surviving Spouse
$5,250	$0	$3,500

This is the doubly punishing nature of this government mandated living money machine. You can build a life together and work hard for decades in your marriage, and then death snatches your spouse away and the government takes away a chunk of your retirement income. This is because both spouses must be alive to get the full benefit they have earned. If you die, even while married, your spouse only gets one social security benefit payment per month (the largest of the two checks).

Thankfully, there are smart products we can buy to "maximize" and protect your combined married Social Security income and help mitigate or replace the potential lost income that occurs through the death of a spouse. These strategies work the best for healthy people with good life expectancies. (We'll discuss similar strategies regarding defined benefit pensions in Part 3 of this book.)

An Example: Doctor and Widower

Ron and Molly met in the early 1980s. They fell in love and got married. Then Molly finished her schooling and residency and became Dr. Jones, an excellent medical physician. Unfortunately, the pressures of Dr. Jones' career and other struggles drove Ron and Molly apart. After 12 years of marriage, they divorced around 2004. Since Dr. Jones has earned significant income from the mid-1980s onward, she has been able to max out her social security wage base for the past 35 years (A+ job!).

Over the last two decades, Ron has been married twice and is currently married to his third wife. He is retired now and drawing $2,000 per month at age 70 from Social Security retirement. Out of the blue, Dr. Jones dies. She also had been retired and was receiving $3,800 in Social Security retirement before her death. Ron can "up" his Social Security payment to his former wife's $3,800 monthly benefit as a "vested widower" since he was married to Dr. Jones for more than 10 years.

Unfortunately, many people don't realize you can swap to the higher monthly benefits like this. If you know anyone in a similar situation, please have them contact the Social Security Administration right away. Millions of these dollars go unclaimed each year.

The ability to draw on the benefits of your spouse, or even former spouse, is one more reason to get legally married rather than just cohabitating. Getting married starts the "vesting" for both the spousal benefits and the widow(er)'s benefit. Go to SSA.gov for more information.[26]

Chapter Conclusion

Social Security is far from a perfect system, and there will always be changes in the rules, but if you want to "play the Social Security game," know the rules and maximize the output. If you work a traditional job and get a W-2, do all that you can to increase your income if you're below the Social Security wage base. Think of each year as an exam. Not everyone can get straight A's but try to increase your grade to at least keep up with the ever-inflating social security wage base each year.

If you are self-employed, invest in your business and understand the value of paying more into Social Security during your working years. Don't go for tricks or immediate gratification. If you're fortunate enough to have a successful business with a healthy profit, set your wages close to the SS wage base ($168,600 in 2024) and pay more into Social Security—not less. This extra 15.3% tax may be seen as ridiculous to some, but the extra tax now could give you another $1,000 or more per month in Social Security retirement benefits with a generous cost-of-living adjustment.

Moreover, if you have a joint business with your spouse, it is better to maximize one spouse's wage record instead of splitting your earnings. Like drawing your social security as early as possible (see the next chapter), the math supports taking one "high-grade" income over two lower grade incomes.

---

[26] Do You Qualify for Social Security Spouse's Benefits? August 24, 2023. Social Security Administration. https://blog.ssa.gov/do-you-qualify-for-social-security-spouses-benefits/

Are there better investments than social security retirement? Maybe. Will you find them and be disciplined to contribute regularly? That is doubtful. Even if you invest wisely in other long-term vehicles, social security retirement is forced upon you. You might as well get the best return possible for this government mandated living money machine.

If you have 20 to 30 years left until normal retirement age (age 67 for most readers), please get help from a qualified "defensive" financial planner who will change your paradigm and save more money for retirement. Sacrifice some of today's "gratification" for tomorrow's lifestyle at retirement. Also, pay more Social Security taxes and have a reasonable Social Security strategy. Try to get at least Bs and Cs, not Fs each year in the "wage game."

Personally, at age 69, I do not regret paying max into social security for 35 years so I could receive the max monthly benefit at age 66 for me. Having that automatically hitting my bank account each month is an enormous piece of mind, especially knowing that it's $1,000 to $1,500 more per month than if I wouldn't have played the game.

In summary, you also can enjoy a better retirement by maximizing your Social Security retirement benefit. Sure, Social Security is not a perfect system, but it can be a significant part of your overall retirement portfolio. With smart planning, you can feel good about having a higher base lifetime income with a COLA at retirement. As always, also inquire at www.retirementnationwide.com for more information, and feel free to email me directly at info@retirementnationwide.com for additional details.

Now that we've done the hard work of maximizing our social security wages during our working years, the next chapter focuses on when to start drawing our hard-earned Social Security retirement.

Disclaimer: The facts and numbers presented within this chapter are based on Social Security publications as of 2024. These numbers will change in future years, and it is your responsibility to track these changes that may affect your benefits. Please go to SSA.gov for more information.

2-C: Social Security: When to Draw?

At the time of this book, I had spent 40+ years in the financial planning business. The biggest discussion and even controversy over my years has to do with when to draw your Social Security income. Most people can't draw on Social Security until they hit their 60s. The only exception is someone who becomes disabled. If disabled per the Social Security Administration's definition, you can draw your benefit at whatever age you are at what is called your 'disability onset date.' We won't discuss disability in this book. Focusing purely on social security retirement, what are the possible ages you can draw?

Age 60. At age 60, you can draw a widow(er) benefit based on your spouse's income if you were married for a year or more at the time of your spouse's death or if you were married for 10 years or more to a past spouse who since passed away or married at least a year to you current spouse.

Age 62. At age 62, you can draw a reduced benefit amount (about 30% lower than age 67[27]). Your benefit will also be less depending on your earned income. If you earn less than $22,320 income in the 2024 year, you won't get an income-based benefit reduction. If you earn more, you may get hit by a $1.00 loss for every $2.00 earned above that threshold. Taking social security at age 62 is NOT recommended for full-time employees or partners in partnerships with substantially more W-2 income than the threshold.

Age 66 to just before 67. The year that you reach normal retirement age (NRA), you can make $56,520 of W-2 income before your social security retirement benefit is reduced $1.00 for every $3.00 of earned

---

[27] Starting Your Retirement Benefits Early. https://www.ssa.gov/benefits/retirement/planner/agereduction.html

income above that limit. If your birthday is early in the year, you might be able to draw in January with no reduction (depending on your income).

Age 67. Age 67 is currently the normal retirement age (NRA) for those born in 1960 or after. This age will likely go up in the future. For now, at age 67, you can draw your Social Security without fear of any penalty based on your earned income. You can even earn hundreds of thousands of dollars each year with no effect on your social security retirement monthly benefit (although such a high income will mean 85% of your social security income is subject to Federal income tax).

Age 67+ to 70. For each month you delay drawing benefits beyond your normal retirement age (age 67 for many), you get a certain percentage increase in your benefits (technically called 'Delayed Retirement Credits'; each month delayed is 2/3 of 1%, which equals 8% for a full year deferred). That increase stops once you hit age 70, at which time you will have earned exactly 24% (three years at 8%) more than if you took your benefits at age 67.[28]

Age 70+. There is no reason why you would want to delay claiming your benefits past age 70 because your benefit amount will not increase any further, except for inflation adjustments.

Live Well: Do the Math

As you can see from the above age descriptions, there is a wide range of about 10 years between age 60 and age 70 where you can possibly draw your social security retirement benefits. There is also the appeal of waiting to draw your benefits to accrue a higher monthly benefit. But if you delay, you miss out on a big chunk of money each month. These issues are why it can be very confusing to decide when to draw your benefits.

For instance, many people are being advised that delaying is the right idea in the long term. They do what Social Security recommends and "defer to make more." The Social Security Administration is eager

---

[28]   How Delayed Retirement Affects Your Social Security Benefits. https://www.ssa.gov/benefits/retirement/planner/1960-delay.html

also to tell you to delay because that puts less stress on an already overburdened system. I don't believe their recommendation to wait as long as possible is given out of a concern for what is best for you, sad to say. Since the government advises this "delayed" strategy, aren't you at least concerned?

I've even heard the 8% increase per year between age 67 to 70 be called an "8% rate of return" by Social Security employees doing workshops. The benefit increase is NOT an 8% compounded yield (rate of return). It is just "simple interest," totaling 24% if you defer a full three years (for people born on or after 1960). Also, to get that full 24% simple interest "multiplier" you are forgoing three years (for people born on or after 1960) of monthly benefits and three years of cost-of-living (COLA) increases. The monthly benefits and COLAs can add up to losing hundreds of thousands of dollars. To prove this, let's introduce a case study.

Joe is a great guy. He worked hard as a machinist for most of his career. His coworkers loved his carefree attitude and steadfast work ethic. None of that information is relevant to the numbers. What matters now is that Joe is finally hitting age 67 and ready to welcome a hard-earned Social Security retirement. Like millions of others, he now must decide about his Social Security retirement. Joe can get a $2,000 per month benefit if he draws at age 67, his normal retirement age. If he waits until he is age 70, he will get $2,480 per month, which is $480 more every month. Before Joe gets too excited about this $480 increase each month three years later, he needs to DO THE MATH to determine if that enticing $2,480 per month is worth waiting three years for. The required math is based on first calculating Joe's breakeven point.

If Joe waits, then he gets a big fat zero dollars in benefits month after month for up to three years. If he chooses to take the $2,000 right when he turns 67, then he gets $2,000 multiplied by 36 months, which equals $72,000 (not factoring in cost-of-living adjustments, which he will get at the start of each new calendar year). That's a lot of money to not receive.

To make the math easier, let's say Joe's birthday is at the end of December. Thus, he would receive $24,000 in year one, 2025. Then let's give him a 4% cost-of-living increase (based on estimated inflation). Now he gets $2,080 per month for year two (2026), which equals $24,960. In year 3 (2027), he gets a 5% COLA increase, meaning he gets $2,184 per month, which equals $26,208. Now, finally he turns 70 at the start of 2028. We'll assume a 6% COLA increase, meaning he gets $2,315 (rounded) for January 2028. This is the month when he would have started his "defer to draw more" max social security retirement benefit, but he would have missed out on the following money:

Year 1, 2025: $24,000

Year 2, 2026: $24,960

Year 3, 2027: $26,208

Total: $75,168 received by the time Joe turns 70.

Granted, if Joe waited until age 70 (January 2028) to draw his Social Security retirement, he would receive more than the $2,480 per month we originally calculated. This is because a "separate" cost-of-living adjustments get added to a person's social security benefit each year even if they don't draw on that benefit yet. These yearly adjustments are usually smaller (and sometimes zero) compared to the post-retirement cost-of-living adjustments. These specific adjustment rates aren't made publicly available, so we can only guess that Joe might be getting about $2,600-$2,700 if he waits until age 70. Let's use $2,650.

Thus, in January 2028, Joe would either get $2,315 (rounded) or $2,650 (estimated). Who wouldn't take the larger amount? Well, do not forget the cool $75,000+ that Joe would have already collected by starting at age 67! How long does it take to break even on $75,000 missed benefits if you only get a mere $335 more a month? Divide that $335 into $75,000. This is almost 224 months, which is about 18.7 years. This means Joe needs to live to just shy of age 89 to make up for the lost $75,000 he would have collected in those first three years from age 67 to 70. Maybe he's ok with "betting" on that.

However, the age 89 breakeven point is not the full picture because the $75,000 can also be wisely invested or directed to keep earning money year after year. This means, it takes much, much longer to just break even. For instance, say Joe didn't need the $2,000 monthly benefit when he first began to draw at age 67. Rather, he invested the money. Let's go with a meager 4% return to play it safe.

Let's make the math cleaner and say that the first year he invests about $20,000 of his $24,000 (perhaps the rest went to taxes). The same goes for the next two years: he invested $20k and $20k more. He presumably can afford to do this because if he was considering the choice of not taking social security at all until age 70, then he likely didn't need the money to pay essential life expenses.

If Joe took the $70,000 ($20k for three years plus interest) and purchased an immediate annuity for a 70-year-old male, it would pay out over $500 per month. This $500 is greater than the $335 reduction of his benefits for taking them at age 67 instead of age 70. Even with larger COLAs on the larger age 70 check ($2,650 per month), when we factor in the "time value of money," Joe's true "real dollar breakeven age" would be beyond age 100!

Therefore, Joe needs to live to age 100 to truly break even (with "present value assumptions") on his decision to wait three more years to draw his social security retirement benefits. What is the percentage of men who live to be 100? You might become depressed if you look it up; it isn't very high. Thus, our hard-working and fun-loving Joe could easily lose out on a bunch of money if he just goes along with the common thinking of the day to "defer and make more." Does he really want to play the odds that he'll live not just to 89 (his breakeven if he never invests his $60k) but to 100 years old (if he smartly invests in something like an annuity at age 70)?

I could even dare to say that the Social Security Administration recommends people like Joe wait to draw precisely because they know the odds are in their favor: most people will sadly pass away before they ever make up for the lost monthly benefits they would have received if they had started drawing at their normal retirement age. Remember, if Joe dies before age 70, ZERO benefit would have been paid, although the spousal survivor benefit would be a little higher.

This is why I say that advisors or planners who think delaying is better almost certainly haven't done the math. Don't believe even your advisor who recommends waiting without getting a second or third opinion. This could mean hundreds of thousands of dollars lost.

More than just lost income, it is also important to consider quality of life. We all slow down as we age, and the years of 65ish to 75ish are usually your much healthier and more active years than 75ish to 85ish. This means it would be much better for you to have some extra income earlier in your sixties and seventies to help you travel, go on vacations, and enjoy your life how you see fit before health problems stop you. The focus is on the financial numbers in this book, but also consider the extra value of having more income in your earlier retirement years. These early years are the "quality of life" years. These are our "Go Go Years"...Tom Hegna.

Age 62 versus Age 67

We can take Joe's example even further. If it is better for him to draw at age 67 than at age 70, what about drawing even sooner? Recall that Joe can be eligible for drawing Social Security retirement at age 62. There are two disadvantages to drawing before normal retirement age. You get hit with a percentage reduction in benefits (although less than 8% extra for waiting) you also get hit by a benefit reduction if you earn too much money each year before reaching normal retirement age.

The percentage reduction is important. Here is a simple table showing rough numbers:

Age	% Reduction	Joe's Benefit
62	70%	$1,400.00
63	75%	$1,500.00
64	80%	$1,600.00
65	87%	$1,740.00
66	93.3%	$1,866.00
67	100%	$2,000.00

If Joe stopped working (or earned less than $22,320, using 2024's number), then he would get $1,400 per month if he decided to draw at age 62. This would be his locked in benefit for the rest of his life, plus the cost-of-living adjustments each year. To recap, the full range for Joe is:

Age	% Change	Joe's NRA Benefit	Joe's Actual Benefit
62	70%	$2,000.00	$1,400.00
63	75%	$2,000.00	$1,500.00
64	80%	$2,000.00	$1,600.00
65	87%	$2,000.00	$1,740.00
66	93.3%	$2,000.00	$1,866.00
67	100%	$2,000.00	$2,000.00
68	108%	$2,000.00	$2,160.00
69	116%	$2,000.00	$2,320.00
70	124%	$2,000.00	$2,480.00

The age 62 monthly benefit of $1,400 is significantly less than the age 70 monthly benefit of $2,480 (about 56% less), but we yet again must use the power of MATH to decide if the large reduction at age 62 is worth it. Clarification: we won't use actual inflation numbers for the past years. Rather, we'll use a standard 4% cost-of-living adjustment for ages 62 to 67.

Age	COLA (4%)	+	Monthly	Yearly	Total
62			$1,400.00	$16,800.00	$16,800.00
63	$56.00	+	$1,456.00	$17,472.00	$34,272.00
64	$58.24	+	$1,514.24	$18,170.88	$52,442.88
65	$60.57	+	$1,574.81	$18,897.72	$71,340.60
66	$62.99	+	$1,637.80	$19,653.62	**$90,994.22**

Over the years of 62 through 66, Joe will collect about $91k in social security benefits if he draws right when he turns 62. If he waits until he turns 67, then he would draw about $2,200 with 2% inflation factored in. So, his two monthly numbers to compare at age 67 would be about $1,700 (with 4% COLAs) if he starts at age 62 and $2,200 if he waits until normal retirement age at 67. The difference is about $500 per month (estimated since we don't know the Social Security Administration's actual yearly increases when someone delays their benefits).

How many months until that $500 extra overtakes Joe's $91k of prior benefits paid? That would be just over 182 months, or 15-plus years. In other words, Joe would be about 82 years old when he finally starts enjoying his decision to delay drawing social security retirement until full retirement age. That's 15 years later!

Once again, though, this isn't the full picture. The "time value of money" (money in hand is worth more today than tomorrow)[29] needs to step in and make clear that it is FAR more profitable to have $91k accrued at age 67 than to just begin to get an estimated $500 more per month after 15 years. If Joe invested most of his social security benefits every month starting at age 62 up through age 67, even a modest 4% return would mean he would build up over $100,000 (an additional $9,000) when he turns 67. If he purchased an immediate annuity, it would pay him greater than $600 per month, which is larger than the reduction he got hit with for drawing at age 62! Does this make sense?

What if Joe Works Past Age 62?

One thing that certainly means you shouldn't take Social Security retirement early is if you decide to continue working full-time. If you've got a great job (or business) that you love, you likely will keep earning a good income from age 62 to 67. This means you might get hit very hard by the Social Security Administration's reduction in benefits based on income. To review, if you draw benefits before your normal retirement age and earn over a certain annual amount ($22,320 in 2024), your benefits are reduced by $1 for every $2 you earn above that annual limit.

If our buddy Joe wanted to keep working as a machinist, then he wouldn't want to draw until he was either ready to retire from his job or he reached normal retirement age at age 67. To prove this, let's say Joe makes $80,000 per year at age 62 and beyond. Using 2023 numbers, his excess $58,760 wages would mean his benefits are reduced by $29,380 (in 2023). This is GREATER than both his reduced early draw monthly benefits and his normal retirement benefit of $24,000 per year. This means he would get NO benefit payments from the Social Security administration if he drew before age 67, but he would still suffer the lower benefit payment for unwisely deciding to draw early. If you're

---

[29] Time Value of Money Explained with Formula and Examples. Investopedia.com. https://www.investopedia.com/terms/t/timevalueofmoney.asp.

curious to test your own scenarios, the SSA has an online Retirement Earnings Test Calculator you can use.[30]

The Best Age to Draw Social Security

After covering so many things, here is my simple conclusion. **The best time to draw your social security retirement benefit is as soon as you can UNLESS you will get hit with a penalty for working too much.** Therefore, you can't really know if drawing at age 62, age 67, or somewhere in between is the best until you reach age 62 and truly know if you want/need to keep working. If you have a great job that you don't mind, keep working and wait to draw until age 67. Remember, there is never an income-based reduction on your benefits once you reach normal retirement age (67 for most). So, once you reach 67, all the prior math regarding the time value of money is valid. Don't ever delay your benefits beyond age 67 unless you really like to gamble and just know you'll live to age 105. What if you're wrong and die early, I would not want to be the financial advisor that recommended "delaying" and my client died early.

As an aside, I have a lot of public employee clients who have great defined benefit pensions. The income from such pensions doesn't affect (reduce) social security retirement benefits, so most of my clients retire at age 62 and draw social security immediately. With those two monthly payments, my clients often see 75-90% of their pre-retirement income during their "go-go" years in the mid-60s and early 70s when "quality of life" is usually the best. We'll return to pension talk in Part 3.

For me personally, of course I followed this advice. I love my job and certainly didn't want to stop helping people (retire) at age 62. I'm still working today, even though I will turn age 70 in 2024. Thus, I couldn't draw social security retirement early at age 62 since my income would have eliminated all my benefits. However, once I turned age 66 (my full retirement age) and was free from the shackles of income-based

---

[30]   Retirement Earnings Test Calculator. SSA. https://www.ssa.gov/OACT/COLA/RTeffect.html

reductions, you better believe that I applied ASAP and started drawing benefits.

I was fortunate to receive the absolute maximum social security benefit possible when I began to draw (because I got A+ grades for 35 out of 40 years by hitting the wage base limit each of those years).[31] Let me share my actual social security benefit numbers with you when I began drawing in October 2020. We'll bring my monthly benefit down to an even $3,000 to make the math easier. See the following table on why I started drawing social security early, and why you should too!

[Jim: this diagram and section needs improvement and may not be correct. – Nick]

	Jim's Personal Age 67 vs. Age 70 Benefit Comparison						
	Waiting until 70						
Monthly Benefit	$0	$0	$0	$0	$3,960	(32% increase**)	
Yearly Benefit	$0	$0	$0	$0	$47,880	**$47,520**	Total Income from 66-70
	Drawing at NRA						
Yearly COLA	--	5.9%	8.7%	3.2%	4.0%***		
Monthly Benefit	$3,000	$3,177	$3,453	$3,564	$3,706		
Yearly Benefit	$36,000	$38,124	$41,441	$42,767	$44,478	**$202,809**	Total Income from 66-70
Age in January	66*	67	68	69	70	**$155,289**	Extra Benefit Income
Benefit Year	2021	2022	2023	2024	2025		

*Normal Retirement age for people born before 1954.
**This 32% increase is 8% x 4 years.
***Estimated COLA for 2025.

Notice how much money I will collect between age 66 and 70. With the COLAs, I will collect $202,809 by the time I reach my maximum age deferral of age 70 in January 2025. My monthly benefit amount will be about $3,706 (cost-of-living adjustments increasing my original $3,000 each year). Had I waited until age 70, my monthly benefit would be 32% higher than my original $3,000, which would be $3,960 ($254 more

---

[31] Workers with Maximum-Taxable Earnings. https://www.ssa.gov/oact/cola/examplemax.html#fnc

per month). That monthly difference would take over 66 years to break even.

Some advisors point out that the normal retirement age (NRA) benefit amount goes up each year, so it offsets the COLA. First off, the NRA increase creeps up at a lower rate than the COLA and in small COLA years doesn't even increase. If the NRA benefit amount increased by 3% each year, my new breakeven point would be over age 100! That doesn't even factor in the time value of money.

Therefore, I believe mathematically that I've personally done the right thing by drawing at normal retirement age (66 for me) and not waiting for my maximum deferral of age 70. I would have drawn Social Security even earlier, but I was still working. My benefits would have been eliminated because of my large, earned income between ages 62 and 66.

I have also done the same math for hundreds of people. I don't bet that I'll live past age 95, and I also don't believe social security will increase the NRA max benefit amount more than 3% per year. Don't rely on the Social Security website or benefit calculators that don't factor in COLAs and the time value of money (inflation adjusted). Do the math yourself!

Premature Death (Bad Health)

All the calculations so far have been about breakeven points and longevity. What if you decide to postpone drawing your social security retirement benefits anyway? Say that you wait until age 70, but you die before your 70th birthday or shortly thereafter? You will receive little or no Social Security retirement benefits personally (although a surviving spouse may get some of yours if he or she draws on your record). Therefore, it is especially important to draw early if you know you are in bad health and at higher risk for premature death.

In my Social Security workshops, I tell the story of a man at his 70th birthday party. To celebrate, a huge cake has been made with literally 70 candles, glowing brightly lighting up the whole room. This now 70-year-old man gets ready to blow out the impressive 70 candles on his cake and takes several huge breaths. As he starts blowing, he has a sudden heart attack, and his face suddenly smooshes down into that celebratory cake.

Even worse for this poor man, he decided to postpone drawing his social security until age 70. Since this man's normal retirement age was 66, this means he lost out on four whole years of monthly benefits, likely equally over $100k. Why did this man wait to draw until 70? He heard that waiting is what "got him the most money," and his financial planner told him that his biggest problem was "living too long," not dying too soon. If the planner is wrong in this recommendation, then what?

Will his financial planner reimburse him for that lost $100k? Not a chance. And yet there is a chance, even if it is low, that this scenario could happen to anybody. We all want to live long lives, especially in our 'golden years' of retirement. But death can hit us hard at any time. Especially if you have known health conditions, waiting to draw your social security is playing with financial fire.

Remember, when you see a life-expectancy table showing age 84, that means 50% live beyond that age but 50% die early. 50/50 odds are not good. Why risk it? Get on the Social Security payroll as soon as you can. Not one client of mine has ever come back to me and regretted drawing their monthly benefits early in 40 years of being a financial planner.

Review: Age Ranges

Let me say it again. When is the best time to draw your Social Security income? **My answer: as soon as you can, unless there is a penalty for working too much.** With this in mind, consider the following age ranges again.

Age 60: Draw if you're a widow(er) from your spouse's reduced benefit and have no more wages (you can have interest earnings, pensions, etc.—just not more earned income than the threshold. Then at age 62, you can take the higher of your personal Social Security benefit or the widow(er) benefit.

Age 62: Draw if you can get your earned income down to less than the $22,320 threshold for 2024 (this threshold will likely go up every year). If you want to work more and your earned income is over the threshold, just draw as soon as you quit or reach your normal retirement age (age 67 for those born in 1964 or after). Go with the sooner of the two.

NRA (Age 67 for most): Draw at your NRA no matter what! Many advisors (and Social Security—see SSA.gov) will try to convince you to wait to age 70 for the 8% per year increase (up to 24% more than NRA for those born in 1960 or after). Please research this before you automatically default to waiting until age 70. Call or email me and discuss. As you saw above, I drew my social security at my normal retirement age of 66 (at the end of 2020/start of 2021) while making substantial income and since then have received COLAs (cost-of-living adjustments) of 1.3%, 4.9%, 8.7%, and 3.2% (in 2021, 2022, 2023, and 2024). The math shows that even with 4% COLAs in the next 2 years, the breakeven point of waiting until I was age 70 would be past age 100. Look at the math yourself. Even if you're not a "math person," make sure your advisor will do this math for you or find a better "defensive" planner who will do that.

Spousal Considerations

We have looked at when to draw social security retirement, but we also know that social security is a living money machine because the day you die, your benefit stops. If you're single and have no dependents, that abrupt stop may be your plan, but what if you have a spouse or children?

We won't focus on children in this book, but be aware that a child can draw benefits on a parent's social security wage record if that parent dies and no spouse is also going to draw on that deceased parent's record. The child can get benefits until age 18 or graduate from high school. Then the benefits would stop (called a black-out period). [32]

---

[32] Drawing on a parent's record can also happen if the parent begins receiving social security disability benefits, but the topic of social security disability is also beyond the scope of this book.

Returning to spouses, if you are married and one of you is receiving Social Security retirement, the other one is entitled to the spousal benefit even if you're married for just one year. If you're cohabitating and your domestic partner is receiving a social security retirement check of, say, $2,000 per month, why not get married and a year later start receiving $1,000 per month (50% if you're at NRA)?

Secondly, two people receive two checks, but once your spouse dies, the survivor gets the larger of the two checks (assuming both are at NRA). This was discussed in the last chapter. What wasn't discussed is the substantial reduction for most retirees, especially if social security is one of your main sources of income.

I recommend evaluating the budget of the surviving spouse and determining if you should give up some income or assets today to protect the income for the surviving spouse. The financial planning industry calls this concept social security maximization.

Social Security Maximization

Social security maximization is a concept of protecting the surviving spouse from the large reduction after the first death and maybe after both deaths if an estate value is desired for children of other heirs.

Example 1:

Spouse A receives $2,500 per month from social security and spouse B receives $2,500 per month (or close to A's benefit). The total would be $5,000 per month or $60,000 per year plus generous COLAs (8.7% in 2023) based on inflation. So, when either A or B dies, the benefit would be cut in half. Either A or B as a survivor only gets ONE check of $2,500/month or $30,000 per year. That's a big reduction of 50%.

Example 2:

Spouse A receives $3,000 per month and spouse B $2,000 per month. That's also $5,000 per month or $60,000 per year. However, here the survivor would get the larger of the two checks or $3,000 per month. That's still $2,000 less (a 40% reduction).

Example 3:

Spouse A gets $3,400 per month and spouse B never contributed to social security. At NRA, Spouse B will take 50% of spouse A's benefit ($1,700 per month, assuming they have been married a year or over). That's $5,100 per month ($61,200 per year). The survivor receives the largest check (at NRA) of $3,400 per month ($40,800 per year). This is still a reduction of $20,400 (33%).

How do you make up for this lost income?

If you have substantial assets that are accumulating (maybe tax-deferred), you can commit assets to income with a product called a SPIA. That is a Single Premium Income Annuity. This will provide more income per dollar of assets for ages 70 and above than RMDs or market distributions, and it's guaranteed for life. All major life insurance companies offer this product.

My mentor and one of the best in the business is Tom Hegna. He wrote an incredible book, *Paychecks and Playchecks: Retirement Solutions for Life*.[33] This is a must-read to explore guaranteed income for life. Here's an example. Let's say you are 70 years old and want to make up the $20,000-$30,000 lost income for your spouse's social security. You can buy this annuity for about $200,000 ($20,000 a year) to $300,000 ($30,000 a year). That's right, this product gives a 10% (or more) payout rate. If you withdraw 10% per year from your IRA or mutual funds, the survivor will probably run out of money before they die. Like Social Security, you cannot outlive a SPIA.

Psychologically, the number one fear of retirees in America is "outliving their money." This is why SPIAs work for at least a portion of your income. The 10% payout rate example is based on the rate at the time of annuitization, but once the asset is converted to income, it's guaranteed by the financial strength of the life insurance company. Think about it.

[33]   Paychecks and Playchecks: Retirement Solutions for Life. Tom Hegna. 2011. Acanthus Publishing. https://www.amazon.com/Paychecks-Playchecks-Retirement-Solutions-Life/dp/098421738X

If you live 20 years, the income would be twice the asset transfer (in the case of $200,000).

Putting $200,000 into a SPIA that pays out $20,000 per year guaranteed for life would provide you a total of $400,000 in 20 years (30 years would be $600,000!). So, then you say, what if I die after a year? What happens to my money? There are several options, and they will be discussed in Part 3: Chapter B of this book when we study private protection plans for defined benefit pensions. In short, you can get annuities that guarantee the entire $200,000 initial investment or more be paid out.

So, what if you don't have the $200,000 of assets to transfer for income? If you're insurable and willing to give up a little of your combined social security income to protect the survivor, you can buy the $200,000 of tax-free cash using life insurance that could buy the annuity for the guaranteed income. This may sound complicated, but, in essence, you're buying permanent life insurance policies from highly rated life insurance companies on each other to make up a portion of the lost social security income from the death of the first spouse. That life insurance proceeds can be converted to guaranteed incomes for life or invested and preserve the principal for the estate.

Planning like this takes time, both in education and professional help from advisors. Like pension option planning (covered in Part 3 of this book), term insurance doesn't work here because only 1-2% of term insurance policies are in force the day you die. If outliving your income is a problem, outliving your "life insurance" should be even more concerning.

A popular radio personality who claims to know life insurance suggests to "buy term and invest the difference," meaning the difference in monthly premiums between permanent life insurance and term. His reasoning is that you won't need life insurance when you're over age 65. Well, at the time of writing, I'm age 69 and have been in the business for over 40 years. I have never met a 65-year-old (or older) person who didn't want some permanent life insurance. What people don't want is to pay the premiums. Many policies today provide lifetime protection with no premiums after age 60 to 65. The younger you are, the better deal this is because it's: **"The only investment you'll ever make where you're discriminated against based on your age and your health."**

If you're going to get advice here, PLEASE see a financial planner or CPA who is not a termite. A A "termite" is someone or companies who only push term life insurance and won't even consider other options. Granted, term life insurance may make sense. For instance, if the problem you are trying to solve will go away in a few years or, say, by retirement, like paying off your mortgage or other debt, college education, income replacement with young kids; then term insurance may be the best solution.

However, there are many uses for permanent life insurance especially when dealing with a <u>problem that won't go away.</u> (You can't fix a permanent problem with a temporary solution.) In fact, some problems get even bigger as you get older. And open-minded CFP, CLU, ChFC, etc. will help you build a life insurance portfolio. See the diagram below, borrowed from my other book, Die Neatly.

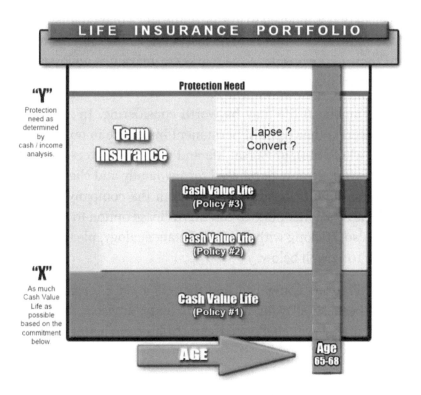

NEEDS (WANTS) for Permanent Life Insurance

There are several places where you should consider building a life insurance portfolio so that you end up in retirement not only with NO MORE PREMIUMS but also tax-free access to the cash value. One philosophy that we have come to accept and preach to our clients is: "Federal Income Tax rates will probably be much higher in the future." My best reference for this is from another financial expert in the financial services world, David McKnight. He wrote a book, *The Power of Zero*, which talks about strategies to possibly get to zero tax bracket during retirement and even have income Tax Free Social Security payments.[34]

Unfortunately, for most of my clients who are public employees with defined benefit pensions, they will never get to a zero-tax bracket at retirement since pension payments are subject to ordinary tax rates. Still, pension recipients can still get a lot lower tax bracket in retirement by purchasing ROTH investment options and LIRPs (see Part 3).

A LIRP (life insurance retirement plan) with today's modern policies that have a yield that is indexed to upside of the stock market upside, but on bad stock market years there are no losses due to the market. Would you give up some of the upside of the market to guarantee no losses due to negative market years?

If so, indexed universal life may be worth considering. In 40+ years and owning several other types of permanent insurance in my personal portfolio (like whole life), universal life and variable universal life, for the past 6 years, I have only purchased for my family and clients either indexed universal life, or term insurance from the company with the best indexed universal life. I like to call this a "lease option to buy" (like Real Estate). Also, sticking with the Real Estate analogy, please see the Life Insurance 101 graph below.

Some of you still aren't convinced that there is a place for permanent life insurance because all your life your parents, advisors, or friends have been termites. I will challenge them to show me better solutions

---

[34]   For a free copy of his book, email me and let's discuss.

for permanent problems than buying "TAX-FREE dollars for pennies a piece."

Think about a $1,000,000 life insurance policy for $20,000 per year for 20 years for a healthy 60-year-old. Why on earth would you possibly buy that policy? I can think of some really good reasons:

1. Pension Option Planning – see Part 3 (Chapter 3-B)

2. Social security Max – see this chapter

3. Estate Tax Liquidity – Wealthy clients for Estate payments "pennies on the dollar"

4. Funding Business Buy/Sell Agreements and Selective Executive benefits

5. Long-Term Care (chronic illness) – if hybrid policy via Accelerated Death Benefit (hybrid plan)

6. TAX-FREE forgivable loans – paid back at death

7. Free from creditors in some states (like Washington State)

8. Final Burial Expenses and funeral costs

Let's say it wasn't called "life insurance" or "whole life" with all of the negative connotations. Let's call it "e-property," and I want to sell you a $1,000,000 piece of "e-property" with the following terms:

1. Zero down!

2. No appraisal, title costs, inspection costs

3. 2% per year (2 cents per $1 per year) for 20 years

4. 20 years – no more payments ($.40/$1)

5. Equity loans of 70% of payments in 10 years (90% in 20 years)

6. Free and clear if death even before the 20-year payment plan – no more payments up death

7. Skip a few years if financial problems – flexible payment.

8. Advance $500,000 for LTC (chronic illness accelerated death benefit), best companies

9. Advance $750,000 if terminally ill (<=12 months to die)-most companies

10. Advance $250,000 for 15 other chronic illnesses like cancer, heart attack, etc. very few companies

[The above list of terms is based on a 60-year-old healthy, non-tobacco user male]

The question is do you want this parcel of e-property? I've asked this for years, and some people answer, "Where is it?" My answer is, "Who cares." It's a contract backed by a Fortune 100 company that is over 140 years old that paid dividends to policy holders through depressions and both World Wars. We put the title in escrow. Ben Feldman, the greatest life insurance agent in history (a non-termite) said, "when you walk out the door, we walk in with Tax Free Dollars for pennies apiece."

Other clients have suggested (usually from their termite advisor) that they can do better investing in the stock market or real estate. My answer: maybe they can do better than the Cash Value of the policy, but what is the rate of return (RoR) on the Death Benefit if you die in 10 years or 20 years?

$300k--	$1,000,000	10 years	RoR=	25% Tax-Free	(32.9% pre-tax equivalent)
$600k--	$1,000,000	20 years	RoR=	5.1% Tax-Free	(6.7%% pre-tax equivalent)

Assumes 24% marginal Tax bracket

It's not supposed to be an investment or even "outperform" those other investments in your portfolio. In contrast, as my good friend and retired master advisor, Rich Hayes, ChFP, CLU, MSFS, says so eloquently, "It's the best financial tool in America today if you know how to use it."

Postponing Retirement Distributions

Before finishing this chapter, let me provide one more example. Take a 67-year-old woman who has a pension and decides to draw her Social Security retirement early based on the math that we already showed in this chapter. She has enough income, but she is curious if the same 'draw earlier' math works for her 403(b)-retirement account (this could also be an IRA, 401(k), 457 plan, etc.). The key is that she can defer the income if it is in her best interest. If someone (you or others) needs the money for your "quality of life," then ignore this math and draw today.

This is different than Social Security retirement for two reasons.

Reason #1

Social security has 8% simple interest increases between normal retirement age and age 70 (age 67 to 70 for most). It is NOT compounded interest. When I heard a social security talk at a National Association of Insurance and Financial Planners (NAIFA) meeting a few years ago, the speaker asked the crowd, "Where else are you going to get an 8% return on your money?" I about had a heart attack on the spot and raised my hand to ask the speaker if he factored in the "time value of money." He froze, and his presentation bombed.

The difference is SIMPLE interest on say $2,000 at 8% is $160. It's $160 every year, not compounding to $173 the next year and so on. Please don't let anyone convince you that the increase in social security is either a "rate of return" or "compounding interest." It is a simple interest calculation to determine how much more you would receive by waiting. However, be sure to factor in all the lost income you give up to wait.

Reason #2

In the retirement asset distribution, you have money compounding tax-deferred while you're waiting to distribute it. This is the true miracle of compounding interest. The only problem is that you are also deferring taxation, and you may move into a higher tax bracket as you wait. Please read the short impactful book, The Power of Zero, by David McKnight to change your paradigm of future tax rate probabilities.

Roth IRAs and LIRPs (Life Insurance Retirement Plans) are the only two vehicles left to compound tax-deferred and withdraw more than the basis TAX-FREE. David does an incredible job of making this argument, so I will defer to him.

		Retirement Plan 7% Rate of Return 4% Withdrawal Amount		
		Withdrawals at Age 67	Deferred Withdrawals to Age 70	Deferred Withdrawals to Age 72
Start	Account Balance	$500,000	$613,000	$701,000
Age 67	Income	$20,000	0	0
Age 70	Income	$21,200	$24,500	0
Age 72	Total Income	$83,673	$24,500	0
Age 73	Total Income	$106,000	$49,745	$28,000
Age 73	Account Balance	$580,000	$650,000	$722,000
	Total	**$686,000**	**$699,745**	**$750,000**
	Excess	--	**$16,745**	**$64,000**

Although these are simplified numbers, you can see that deferring will give more compounding results. This is just at a modest 7% rate of return. The difference is even greater with 8, 9, or 10% growth. However, this doesn't factor in the need for income, the time value of money, or risks associated with the market.

Social security retirement is different. The extra benefit amount you get for delaying past your normal retirement age is NOT compounded growth. It is SIMPLE interest at 8% per year, for three years maximum up to age 70 for those born in or after 1960. Instead of letting it grow at SIMPLE interest, you could draw your benefits early and invest the benefits in COMPOUDING interest rate investments.

In summary, by comparing deferred income of social security versus an investment portfolio, I would strongly advise you to have your financial adviser look at the math between age 67 (normal retirement age) and age 73 (the age of Required Mandatory Distributions from qualified money—401(k), traditional IRAs, TSAs, etc.).

Do the math to decide if you want to draw Social Security retirement early and wait as long as possible to draw out of your other compounding interest retirement funds. In other words, take Social Security retirement as early as possible (except if you earn too much income), and wait as long as possible for investments that have RMDs. Study the math and the consequences of waiting to draw Social Security retirement, and the possible ulterior motives of advisors.

This can get complicated. Seek more than one opinion. I stand by my math on the time to draw Social Security (as soon as you can without penalty). I will debate this with any advisor.

Chapter Conclusion

We've covered a lot of material in this chapter. To wrap it up, I want to offer my personal perspective and repeat a few important things. I'm age 69 and have been drawing my Social Security since age 66 and my wife has been taking the spousal benefit (50% of my benefit) since she was 64. For the past two years, we've received COLAs (cost of living adjustments) of 4.9%, 8.7%. and 3.2% , I almost certainly wouldn't have broken even in my lifetime if I waited to draw! Did you get that advice?

The reason I wouldn't break even in my lifetime is because of the lost income between age 66 and age 70 (my monthly benefit and the years COLA increases). Once again, never underestimate the power of the time value of money (TVM): today's dollars are worth more than tomorrow's dollars because of inflation. Besides making a great decision for our family, we also love the additional $50,000+ benefit income we receive while I'm still working. Gotta love that "wake-up money" along with my three-monthly defined benefit pension deposits (see more of my pension story in Part 3).

As noted, many advisors and the Social Security Administration are adamant that you should wait until age 70 because of the longevity risk of living too long. As you know, waiting extra years to draw gives you 8% additional income for every year from NRA (normal retirement age) up to age 70. We already did the math to show you that gaining an

8% simple interest increase isn't worth GIVING UP all those years of thousands upon thousands of benefit dollars.

Please learn and calculate the breakeven point for yourself. Too many financial planners "drink the Kool-Aid" without doing the math. Major life insurance companies have also preached this DELAY philosophy. I don't get why unless they want don't to sell financial products during that delay gap.

To close out, here are some actual results. My mother-in-law passed away last year at age 92. She became a widow at age 58, and I argued with my in-laws as to why she should take the widow's benefit at age 60 vs waiting until her normal retirement age of 65. My in-laws relented, and she drew at age 60. This was in the early 80's. We had hyperinflation during this time, and in 5 years her benefit was larger than if she waited because of the COLAs! After receiving Social Security retirement for 32 years, she drew tens of thousands of dollars more than if she had waited. This gave her a better lifestyle, and there were no regrets from anyone.

Personally, I know I have done the right thing by drawing early. More importantly, I have never had one client ever come back to me and wish that they would have delayed receiving Social Security retirement benefits. I have done the math for 100s of people and even contradicted their financial advisors. Please study this. Do the math. Research of both sides (draw early or delay). Establish what is best for this financial decision that will go all the way to the grave with you.

PS: Some of you may disagree with me on this, and I welcome your e-mails and rebuttal. I have challenged advisors for years (ask me for my PowerPoint with even more reasons to draw early). Just beware, many who have tried to convert me have ended up being "converted" themselves. And they and their clients are glad about it! Please respond- Jim@retirementnationwide.com.

Part 3

Defined Benefit Pensions

3-A: Introducing Defined Benefit Pensions

In Part 1 of this book, we defined Human Life Value and declared that you are your largest financial asset. We also introduced the concept of a money machine to illustrate your irreplaceable ability to live and earn a living. In Part 2, we explained how Social Security retirement acts as a living Money Machine for Life tied to your lifetime earnings record.

In addition, you can 'spin up' other money machines. For instance, as you work and build a career, some employers will offer you benefits that continue to produce income for you after you stop working. Examples are retirement accounts and exercised stock options. These are wonderful, but they don't qualify as living money machines because they aren't tied to your physical life. In other words, if you die, your retirement and investment accounts continue (and go to designated beneficiaries or are distributed per your will or through your estate).

Like social security retirement, a defined benefit pension is linked to your ability to work through the years. Both Money Machines for Life pay out at retirement based on your years of work and earnings. The biggest difference between the two is who qualifies. As noted at the start of Part 1, nearly all workers in America can qualify for social security retirement if they report wages for at least 40 quarters. Defined benefit pensions, on the other hand, are offered by only a very small percentage of employers in America.

Consider some history. Thirty years ago, almost every major corporation had defined benefit pensions. Today, less than 7% of corporations still have them. Those of you that have such a pension, count on your blessings. Very few people get this kind of guaranteed income for life after retirement! If you do have a pension, I can't emphasize enough how important your pension is. As a Certified Financial Planner, I feel it is irresponsible (for me and other planners) to not discuss, plan, and integrate future pension incomes into your overall financial strategy. I've been told that for every hour you spend planning your retirement income, it's worth over $1,000 per hour to you.

Even if you don't have a defined benefit pension, it still pays to understand these concepts. I have personally benefited greatly from knowing pensions and helping others. Over my 40+ years in this industry, more than 80% of my business has been with public-sector employees[35] and have helped many advisors in more than a third of US states. Whether military, federal employees, or large corporations that still have defined benefit pensions, my goal before I retire is to help clients in all 50 states.

My Personal Tale of Many Pensions

Where did my love of helping people with pensions come from? It began with my need to help myself. Remember that I started out my working years as a high school math and physics teacher, earning just above $30,000 per year. Despite my modest salary, a large perk of my school job was my pension. Having been a math major in college and kind of a nerd (as a physics teacher), I rigorously studied my pension at the young age of 22.

After examining my Washington State Teacher's Retirement System pension, I figured that if I could double my current $30,000 annual salary and make $60,000, I would then receive $3,000 a month for life at age 52. For a 22-year-old, the idea of 30 years of work to then wake up to $3,000+ guaranteed each month was exciting. Count me in!

Well, the plan changed. As you already read about, my life went in a different direction than teaching; although, my past 40 years have been teaching and coaching clients and advisors. Once, I switched careers and got into the financial services, I extensively studied the compensation package, starting with the salary and commissions. Fortunately, I was still working in the 'old days' of more plentiful defined benefit pensions,

---

[35]   Mostly in Washington, Oregon, Minnesota, California, and Idaho.

and my new employer was also offering a defined benefit pension. My practice of studying pensions that began as a teacher continued to pay dividends.

I quickly realized I could put in so many years of employment to maximize my pension. Then I could go to another company and build up another pension (and even another after that). Fast forward 40+ years. After helping so many others with their pensions and other financial goals, I had retired from two fortune 100 companies with 3 separate defined benefit pensions. This was by careful design. What a relief it is every month to have multiple sources of "wake-up money" hit my bank account. I only wish my private company pensions had COLAs (Cost of Living Adjustments) like most public employee's pensions have today. Do not underestimate the compounding power of COLAs.

Regardless, you know I like to make games out of things, and I'm very glad I played the pension 'game' so well. I knew in my 30s that if I could just grow my pension(s) (see the next chapter), I would have a great guaranteed monthly income at retirement by combining my monthly pensions deposits and my social security benefits. This solid base would ensure that even if the stock market crashed or was extra volatile, I would be set for life. This is because both Social Security and my pensions were guaranteed to never decrease for as long as I lived, and I can't outlive the income.

Sample Pension Calculations

Having heard my pension story, let's look closer at the numbers to get a better idea how defined benefit pension math works. Note that the exact calculations vary but most are based on the concept of a percentage rate multiplied by years of service (YOS) multiplied by Average Final Compensation (AFC).[36]

YOS is easy to understand; it is your number of qualifying years of work (usually greater than 1,000 hours in a year). AFC is trickier. It can also be known as Final Average Salary (FAS) or Final Average Compensation

---

[36] Pension Basics: How Pension Benefits Are Calculated. Retrieved August 15, 2019. Equable.org. https://equable.org/pension-basics-how-pension-benefits-are-calculated/

(FAC). Whatever the name, the idea is that the pension picks a few certain years to set as your compensation amount. For government pensions, some states use the average consecutive years earnings of your last three or five years before retirement. Other states use the highest three, or five years, average earnings of your whole employment at that institution.

Once you have your YOS and AFC (or equivalent), a multiplier is used to determine the dollar amount of your yearly pension. A 2% multiplier is common. Consider a hypothetical example with easy math. Greg worked 30 years at the same government job. His final five years of work earned him a salary of $80,000 per year (realistically he'd get COLA increases each year, but let's ignore those). We take 30 years multiplied by 2%, which equals 60%. Then we multiply that by $80,000, which equals $48,000. To determine the monthly amount, we just divide that dollar amount by 12 months, which equals $4,000 per month FOR LIFE!

To verify our math, we can also double-check with what is called the 'Replacement Ratio' for our pension. This rate is the percentage of your AFC that you'll get at retirement. To calculate Greg's Replacement Rate, take his 30 years of service and multiply it by 2%. This equals 60%. Hence, Greg should get 60% of the average of his final years (or highest years) of earnings. Recall that he retired at $80,000 yearly income. What is 2% of $2.4 million? It is $48,000. This proves our math ties out, and Greg can rest easy knowing he will receive a nice pension amount every month after his long, hard 30 years of public service.

Let's now look at some real-life example pension calculations for various jobs with defined benefit pensions.

Role & State	Pension Plan	Pension Calculations
Teacher in Washington	WS TRS2	2% x YOS x AFC (highest 5 average)
Fireman in Idaho	PERSI	2.3% x YOS x AFC (highest 42 months average)
Sheriff in Washington	LEOFF	2% first 15 YOS 2.5% 16-25 YOS x YOS x AFC (highest 5 years) 2% thereafter
Teacher in California	CALSTERS	2.4% x YOS x AFC (highest 3 years)
Boeing Employees	Boeing Pension	1.5% x YOS x AFC (highest 3 years)
Minnesota Police & Fire	PERA Minn	3% x YOS x AFC (highest 5 years)

Notice the percentage multipliers above range between 1.5% and 3%. Remember that we can take each of these percents and multiply them by the years of service to get the Replacement Rate. Consider a teacher in California named Sally. She gets 2.4% of her salary for each year worked. If she works 20 years, we expect the Replacement Rate to be 48% of the average for her three highest years of earnings. So, she can expect to get close to 50%, which makes the math easy.

Pensions do get complicated quickly, especially in the private sector. Other pensions (such as union pensions) have contribution rates for each paycheck. The formula is something like each unit purchased times the number of hours. It is similar, but the contribution rate may change based on the union negotiations. I recommend starting a file for your pension and obtaining a benefit estimate every year to help you compare and track growth annually (perhaps use a spreadsheet if you're so inclined).

There are also defined benefit pensions in the private sector for highly compensated employees that offer 100% replacement income for life. Wouldn't that be nice? We won't address them in this book because they are very rare (and amazingly costly).

Another Example: A Police Chief

Consider another example. Paul is a police chief in the state of Washington. He joined the force right out of college at age 23 and worked his way up to the top through much dedication. After 30 years of service, he is ready to retire at age 53 and enjoy more time to relax, volunteer, and perhaps do some part-time consulting work as a security expert. His pension rules determine his Average Final Compensation (AFC) to be $200,000 per year.

The rules also break apart his years of service into three groups (as of 2023), each with their own multiplier rates. The first 15 years is 2%. The next 10 is 2.5%, and the remaining 5 years are back to 2%. Thus, he has three separate replacement rates (30%, 25%, and 10%) that we add together to get his final replacement rate (65%). Then we can simply take his AFC of $200,000 and multiply it by 65%, which equals $130,000. You can also reach that calculation by using 30 YOS x 2%, equaling 60%. Plus, add 5% for the 15-25 years (15-25 rule: 65% replacement).

An alternate way to calculate the math is to determine the dollar amount of each group of years of service. To do this, use his three percentage multipliers and times them by $200,000.

- 30% of $200k is $60,000.

- 25% of $200k is $50,000.

- 10% of $200k is $20,000.

Then add the $60,000, $50,000, and $20,000 together to get the total pension of $130,000.

The formula:		
(2% x 15 YOS = 30%)	30% x $200k = $60,000/year	
(2.5% x 10 YOS = 25%)	25% x $200k = $50,000/year	
(2% x 5 YOS = 10%)	10% x $200k = $20,000/year	
	Total Pension: $130,000/year	
	/12 = **$10,833/month**	

Paul the police chief has certainly earned such a great pension after so many years serving the community. Better yet, this $130,000 yearly pension will be increased at the end of each year by a cost-of-living adjustment. How big is that pension with a modest 2.5% cost-of-living adjustment?

$200,000/year AFC Police Chief Yearly Pension with COLAs				
Year	Age	Monthly	Annually	Total Income
1	53	$10,833	$130,000	$130,000
6	58	$12,257	$147,083	$830,406
11	63	$13,868	$166,411	$1,622,851
16	68	$15,690	$188,279	$2,519,429
21	73	$17,752	$213,020	$3,533,826
26	78	$20,084	$241,013	$4,681,522
31	83	$22,724	$272,684	$5,980,035

Notice once again the power of cost-of-living adjustments. After 15 years of pension income, Paul is 68 years old (just over normal retirement age for social security retirement - see Part 2), and his monthly pension income has gone up over 50%, from $10,833 at the start to $15,690 in year 16. If he is blessed to live to 78, his monthly pension income will have doubled after 25 years, to $20,084 at the start of year 26. How's that for a living money machine? It's very powerful!

Chapter Conclusion

Hopefully you can see why pensions are so important for those who have them. For most of my public service clients, their defined benefit pension is their largest retirement asset by far, even for those who have over $1,000,000 in their state or local 457 deferred compensation retirement plans. I've always said to my public employee friends and clients that you could make more money (higher salary) in the private sector, but because of the very expensive defined benefit pensions, most private corporations have switched to 401(k) matches which become very little risk and cost to them to manage compared to the pensions. They don't have to guarantee "replacement income."

So, before you leave for "greener private sector pastures," factor in the present value of your lost defined benefit pension if you quit. Your pension is a great reason to stick around. The public sector can't afford to pay you what you're worth, but those defined benefit pensions create wonderful "wake-up" money at retirement. Bottom line: a pension money machine is worth a significant amount!

In the next chapter, we will discuss strategies to increase your pension.

3-B: Increasing Your Defined Benefit Pension

What do you do if you want a larger pension? Work longer to increase your years of service (YOS) and make more money to increase your Average Final Compensation (AFC). These points are obvious, but being reminded of how your pension works can help motivate you.

Remember, specific pension benefit calculations are subject to change, but changes are usually only for new employees. Longstanding employees almost always get 'grandfathered in' with their old pension rules. If your company is going through changes, that is even more reason to study your pension and plan to make it a big part of your retirement income.

Perhaps your spouse or partner has a 401(k) plan, profit sharing plans, IRAs, etc. The balances of these accounts are based on the investment yields within the plan. The longer the money is in the plan, the bigger the return in most cases (thanks to the miracle of compounding interest). But this balance is usually dependent on stock market performance and can be very volatile. The money grows tax-deferred and is available after age 59 ½ (sometimes earlier) without penalty. You just pay income taxes on the withdrawals after age 59 ½.

These kinds of retirement plans can be great vehicles to accumulate a lot of retirement income wealth. However, they can't guarantee money for the rest of your life (unless there is some kind of Guaranteed Lifetime Income Annuity as part of your retirement plan).

The nice thing about these public defined benefit pensions is the ease of calculation. It's just math. Your pension doesn't depend on the interest credited to your account (unless you quit early and withdraw money). It also doesn't depend on the stock or bond market, or the economy. It only depends on three factors:

1. Your years of credited service (YOS)

2. Your Average Final Compensation (AFC)

3. Any early retirement penalties

Example 1

I have a client who was a Superintendent of a small school district, making $180,000 per year. He had 26 Years of Service in the state of Washington and was planning on retiring at age 60. At 57, he had the opportunity to go to a bigger school district and make $220,000 per year, but he still wanted to retire at age 60. After some good planning and sorting out the numbers, he gave the new school district his commitment for 5 years of work. Why five years, despite his desire to retire in three years at age 60? The reason for 5 years is the high-5 pension! Let's suppose he gets no salary increases for simpler math.

Age 60 Retirement	29 YOS								
	Highest 5 Years	$160,000	+	$160,000	+	$220,000	+	$220,000	+ $220,000
	Divided by 5 (AFC)	$196,000							
	Multiplier Rate	2%							
	Formula	2% x 29 YOS x $196,000 AFC							
	Equals (Yearly)	$113,680							
	Monthly (/12)	$9,473							
	Early Retirement Penalty	6%							
	Monthly Penalty	$568							
	Monthly Amount	**$8,905**							
Age 62 Retirement	31 YOS								
	Highest 5 Years	$220,000	+	$220,000	+	$220,000	+	$220,000	+ $220,000
	Divided by 5 (AFC)	$220,000							
	Multiplier Rate	2%							
	Formula	2% x 31 YOS x $196,000 AFC							
	Equals (Yearly)	$136,400							
	Monthly (H/12)	$11,367							
	Early Retirement Penalty	0%							
	Monthly Penalty	$0							
	Monthly Amount	**$11,367**							
	Difference	**$2,462**		27.6%					

By just working two more years past his goal of age 60 retirement, this superintendent gets $2,462 more dollars every month at retirement FOR LIFE. That is 27.6% more for simply toughing it out for two more years of work.

Takeaways. Most people earn their highest salaries right before retirement. For those with defined benefit pension plans, working a couple extra years might make a big difference in increasing their monthly pension benefits. This is because you get a higher replacement rate when you have higher Average Final Compensation. We saw in our example how two more years of work significantly boosted the monthly pension retirement checks (replacement rate of 62% compared to 48.5%). And I'm sure the school district appreciated this superintendent lending his expertise for two more years.

The superintendent also had no early retirement penalties since he accrued over 30 Years of Service (check with each State and Pension plan for details). He could also begin drawing Social Security retirement (see Part 2) at age 62 when he retires, assuming he doesn't earn too much money from another job. When you factor in Social Security retirement, he likely will have somewhere between 75-85% of his prior monthly paycheck replaced through his pension and monthly social security retirement benefit.

All this means our superintendent will likely never have to work again unless he wants to. All he had to do was put in a final two years of work past his original goal of age 60 retirement.

Example 2

Consider an Idaho patrolman, aged 40. Currently, he has an income of $75,000 with 17 YOS. This patrolman is wondering if he should take a position of Sargeant and possibly earn higher pay. But he loves to hunt and fish and isn't sure about the extra hours and commitment at that higher rank.

Great news. In Idaho, it's the Rule of 80 (for police and firefighters).

That means if your age plus YOS is greater than the number 80, you can retire with no penalty. Let's do the math.

Year	Salary	Age	YOS	Total	Status
2024	$75,000	40	17	57	Not Eligible
2034	$107,800	50	27	77	Not Eligible
2036	$105,000	52	29	81	**ELIGIBLE!**

Thus, our patrolman can retire at age 52 and fish/hunt for the next 20 to 30 years (hopefully). The problem with the 3% raises his AFC (42 consecutive months in Idaho) would be about $105,000. So, the formula is 2.3% x YOS x AFC:

2.3% x 29 x $105,000 = $70,035 per year **($5,836 per month)** for life (plus COLAs).

Is that enough for the patrolman? Maybe it is, but with 3% inflation, that's worth only $4,100 in today's dollars. So, if he takes the Sargeant job with a salary of $90,000, he has the potential to get paid significantly more from his pension in retirement. For instance, if after 5 years as Seargeant, he gets promoted to Deputy Sheriff, making $120,000 per year, he will end up with an AFC of $140,000 instead of $105,000. Look at the new math:

2.3% x 29 x $140,000 = $93,380 per year **($7,783 per month)** for life (plus COLAs).

Those additional years of hard work to become Sargeant and Deputy Sheriff means he gets $1,946 more per month once he retires, which is 25% more retirement income for life. Then again, everybody is different with unique life circumstances. If he needed to cut back on work to take care of aging family members or his spouse, maybe the extra years of grueling work hours and stress on the job wouldn't be worth it. The point is to know the math so you can make an informed decision.

Chapter Conclusion

Play the defined benefit "pension maximization" <u>game</u>. The only two factors that you control to determine your monthly pension are your YOS and AFC. The higher you get those two numbers, the bigger your pension. Try to get promoted. Further your education. Climb the public employee (or private company pension) "ladder" and maximize your monthly retirement pension paychecks.

Note: In playing this game, be careful you don't switch states because each state has its own calculations. Let us help you here. If you must move to another state, it can still work well if planned right.

3-C: Defined Benefit Pensions Maximization Strategies

Having established the immense importance and power of a defined benefit pension and the ways you can increase it in the last two chapters, let's move on to strategies for maximizing your pension. To start, I want to make it clear that you should not wait until the month before you retire to make decisions about your pension options. Far too many pension employees do this, never giving much thought to their pension until they are given a form in their retirement packet. Suddenly they must check some boxes and turn in (or submit online) forms that will drastically affect the rest of their lives.

The biggest question many married pensioners face is regarding their spouses. For starters, if you are married, there are pension laws that require your spouse to have the option of continuing some or all of your pension payments if you happen to die before them. A spouse must be offered at least 50% of your monthly pension amount by law if you decide to elect a spousal survivor option. This is probably your biggest retirement decision as a married couple. What do you and your spouse decide to do? Many retirees make a choice without even realizing they can "shop" around for better ways to take care of their spouse if they die after retirement.

What is the best survivor option to choose? Most pensions provide two options. The first is generally automatic (what happens if you don't make any election) and provides for the same amount that you were receiving to continue to your beneficiary, it is often called "Joint and 100% survivor annuity". The other option gives 50% of the amount you were receiving to your spouse upon your death. It is often called "Joint and 50% survivor." Some pensions have other survivor options, but actuarily, the more you provide to your spouse, the more it will cost you by way of reduction in your monthly retirement benefit.

There is another option: elect to give up any spousal pension benefit. This means if you die, your spouse gets nothing. To elect this option, the law also requires your spouse to agree to this choice in writing. So, what do you choose? The default 50% survivor benefit, the 100%, or to give none at all? Certainly, nobody wants to feel like they aren't taking care of their spouse. This is why most people will simply check the "Joint and 100% survivor" box because giving 50% can feel too small for the spouse and giving zero may feel terrible (and cause marital problems). Indeed, there is a comfort in going with 100% and knowing that the exact same pension benefit will continue if the pension-receiving spouse dies. We call this the LOVE OPTION. The problem is, if you check the 100% survivor option, you might unknowingly stand to lose hundreds of thousands of dollars, give up flexibility, have no equity, and "disinherit" your children.

Picking Spousal Survivor Options

This spousal benefit question is the big elephant in the "pension room." Over 75% of married retirees choose to give 100% of their pension payments to their spouse after their death, but nothing comes for free. Electing any spousal survivor option reduces your pension payment. Electing the 100% spousal option (the LOVE OPTION) reduces your pension payment the most. Confusing? I hope so!

So how do you decide what to pick? You must ask yourself, "Is any survivor option the most economical and flexible method of guaranteeing a survivor benefit for my spouse?" To answer that question, the specifics of your pension plan and survivor options must be examined. The amount of reduction for the benefit option you choose usually varies depending on the relative age of the retiree and his or her beneficiary (spouse). Look at the following condensed table to show some average pension reductions. Let's assume a maximum monthly pension of $3,000 per month, which is what would be paid out if a pensioner had no spouse or the spouse agreed to take no survivor benefit.

Monthly Pension Amounts		
Based on a $3,000 per Month maximum pension payment with no spousal survivorship.		
Age of Spouse	**100% Survivor Option**	**50% Survivor Option**
10 Years Older	$2,800 per Month	$2,850 per Month
5 Years Older	$2,700 per Month	$2,775 per Month
The Same Age	$2,400 per Month	$2,700 per Month
5 Years Younger	$2,250 per Month	$2,625 per Month
10 Years Younger	$2,100 per Month	$2,550 per Month

The reason the pension pays less of a benefit the younger your spouse's age is because a younger spouse has more years to live (on average), so the pension 'bakes the cost into' your benefit by reducing your monthly payments. This is calculated by actuarial math. The end result is you and your spouse get less income, the younger your spouse is. You get hit extra hard if you take the 100% survivor option and have a much younger spouse. Notice the decrease from your maximum $3,000 down to $2,100 with a 100% survivor for a spouse ten years younger than you (a 30% reduction).

Let's illustrate our point by introducing a fictitious couple that we'll use as an example for the rest of this chapter. Mandy is a soon-to-be retiree who has worked in public service for decades and has built up a nice pension. She has a husband, named Mario, the same age as her. They were high-school sweethearts, with many hobbies in common, such as traveling to collect local recipes the world over. When not going on grand trips, they reside in a small town, where both of them were born.

However, Mandy's pension isn't concerned with their human story of life, love, and travel. The pension simply uses cold, hard math to calculate the various pension options Mandy can take at retirement. We'll say she would get $3,000 as a maximum pension benefit, with no spousal benefit. Her 100% survivor option would pay out 80% of the $3,000, which is $2,400 per month. Again, this would mean that if Mandy, God forbid, dies, her husband Mario would get this same $2,400 per month until he dies.

At first glance, taking the 100% survivor benefit and ensuring a consistent $2,400 per month for Mandy and her man makes sense. But what is the real financial cost of losing $600 per month? To review, the three most likely choices are 100% survivor benefit ($2,400), 50% survivor ($2,700), or no survivor benefit at all ($3,000).

	100% Survivor Option		50% Survivor Option		No Survivor Option	
Survivor benefit for spouse	$2,400	per Month	$2,700	per Month	$3,000	per Month
Monthly difference	$600	per Month	$300	per Month	$0	per Month

These are the choices Mandy and Mario will have to consider together as a couple. If Mandy doesn't make a choice, she will automatically get the 50% survivor option (by default with most pensions). We'll come back to our couple soon. First, let's look at the significant reasons to elect the 100% survivor option.

Reasons to Go with any Survivor Benefit Option

Note that your personal benefit reduction may not be as significant as our example above. If your reduction is much less, it may make sense to go with the 100% survivor option. Another great consideration is that there are no extra qualifications for you to choose this 100% benefit. For instance, you don't have to be in good health. We will introduce a pension planning strategy later in this chapter where you get private protection that does require you to go through a qualification process that examines many health factors. Taking the guaranteed 100% spousal pension option could be a valuable advantage if you have health problems (like heart diseases, diabetes, recent cancer, smoker, etc).

Especially if you have medical conditions which are considered life-shortening, taking a survivor option may be the best choice for you. This is because if you were to die shortly after you begin receiving payments, your spouse would hopefully live many years and potentially receive hundreds of thousands of dollars over 5, 10, or more years. You also get peace of mind, knowing that your spouse can receive survivor benefits regardless of either of your wellness.

Moreover, your company's pension benefits are guaranteed by the Pension Benefit Guarantee Corporation Fund, which is an official U.S. government agency.[37] Thus, you can trust that your pension benefits

---

[37] Pension Benefit Guarantee Corporation. https://www.pbgc.gov/about/how-pbgc-operates.

will always be there and outlive both you and your spouse. Another quirk is that some pensions (such as military pensions) require the surviving spouse to be receiving a survivor benefit from the pension to be eligible for post-retirement group medical insurance benefits. If your spouse is planning on getting medical benefits from the pension, find out if this requirement is applicable in your situation before deciding to forgo all surviving spouse options in favor of a private protection plan. I don't know of any state pensions that require that, but the military and Federal Government do have that requirement.

Lastly, it's great to know that your spouse cannot outlive the income. If you were to get a private financial product to replace the pension income for your spouse, there is a chance you don't set it up right. For instance, some retirees do not solve this problem properly, and too little money is available for the spouse's annuity. Truthfully, many people choose the 100% survivor benefit simply because they don't know how to get expert help from qualified "defensive" financial professionals. Few Financial Planners specialize in this Pension Option Planning. PLEASE ask them to seek help, we can do that and both work for you best interest.

In conclusion, the "LOVE OPTION" is the quickest, simplest option that many people choose to simply 'be done with it' and get on with retirement. But at what cost?

Returning to the Reduction Math

Now that I've listed a bunch of strong reasons to forget all this pension math and go with the easy 100% survivor choice, let's return to Mandy and Mario. Recall that Mandy's maximum benefit if she took no spousal survivor option would be $3,000 per month. With the 100% survivor spouse option, she gets $2,400 per month, which passes onto Mario at the same $2,400 upon her death. This $600 reduction from her maximum $3,000 equals $7,200 per year, which is $144,000 after 20 years (with no COLA).

In our example, Mandy is very healthy and expects to live at least 20 years after retirement. Let's say Mandy is blessed to live over 20 more years. What happens if Mario dies first? This is statistically more likely, since most men do die first. It is very important to understand that Mandy would get no use out of the reduced spousal option and would give up the $600 per month for no financial advantage. Over 20 years, that $600 adds up to $144,000. To repeat, the survivor benefit is a permanent reduction in your pension payment. You cannot revert back to the maximum payment once you start receiving your retirement income. This is called "irrevocable" (can't be changed)

If Mandy dies first, nobody will get that $7,200 per year ($600 per month) that was taken out of her pension benefit. Or perhaps Mandy does die first but only after 20 years. Mario would need to live for at least five years to break even (earn back that $144,000 they missed out on for 20 years).

As you can see, there is no single answer to what pension survivor benefit option to take because everyone's situation is different, nobody knows the future, and each pension plan must be studied. For instance, there are many state, Federal, Military, and other pensions that have "pop-up" clauses. This means that if your beneficiary dies first, you get to "pop up" to your maximum benefit. However, there is no refund for the benefits already lost in prior months before the death of your beneficiary.

Limiting Options & Disadvantages

Taking the survivor option can be very limiting. There is no equity accrued for the spousal benefit reduction. This contrasts with private protection plans that can grant you access to the cash value of your account. A surviving spouse option also doesn't allow contingent beneficiaries. If both you and your spouse die, nothing continues to your estate or family. We say, "Your pension disinherits your children or estate." Again, you and your spouse could live a long time and give up a lot of money for a benefit that ceases once you both die.

In our Mandy and Mario example, they gave up $144,000 over 20 years. Then once they both die, their estate doesn't get a dime. The only exception to this is with some pensions wherein if both spouses die before their contributions plus interest are paid out, then the residual is paid to their estate. This death window is usually less than three years after retirement. If you want additional money to go to your estate after both you and your spouse die, your pension benefit is probably not the way to do it.

Many pensions also do not have a cost-of-living adjustment (COLA) in the plan. That is what we assumed with Mandy's pension. Her $2,400 per month would never increase, even over 20 years. With a 3% inflation rate, $2,400 per month would have purchasing power of only $1,329 in 20 years. In other words, with 3% inflation, $2,400 in 20 years will be worth what $1,328 is worth today.

Even if your pension has a COLA built into it, that will mean your COLA-adjusted monthly benefit is smaller if you take the survivor option, lower than the non-COLA maximum benefit. You're electing to receive reduced payments now, which in turn means fewer total dollars to adjust upward each year for the COLA increase. For instance, 3% times $3,000 is $90. 3% times $2,400 is $72. That's just for the first year. Every year after that, the compounding COLA is larger and larger for the "big check" maximum benefit. Regardless, the Federal government and many state pensions have pension "COLA" provisions. Why wouldn't you want the yearly COLA on that maximum check?

The surviving spouse also has limited options once the original pensioner spouse dies. A reduced survivor option states that when you die, if your spouse is living, he or she will only receive a monthly taxable benefit. Recall our example with Mandy. We'll say she lived 20 years after receiving her pension. Tragically, by this time, her husband Mario was already terminally ill. He needs to live at least 5 years to break even and recoup that lost $144,000 from taking the 100% survivor reduced pension. In this case, he might also have very pressing medical bills. He'd love to receive a lump-sum tax-free settlement or an interest payment with the balance paid to the estate. However, neither of these options are available under a pension plan. This can become a very high priority the longer you live.

With the survivor options for most pensions, if you die, your spouse (if living) only receives a monthly taxable lifetime benefit that stops upon his or her death. The exceptions are those pensions with guaranteed period payouts, such as 5-, 10-, or 20-year certain options. But even with those provisions, if you've gone past that guaranteed period, nothing passes to your estate.

Thus, it is very possible for the limitations for a typical defined benefit pension to be too burdensome. The alternative is to purchase what we'll call a Private Protection Plan rather than opt for the survivor pension benefit. The idea is that you take the extra money you bring in from your maximum pension payout ($600 more a month in Mandy's example) and use that monthly extra income to purchase a separate financial product. This is called a Private Protection Plan (PPP) and they offer many different options to beneficiaries, including a lump-sum income tax free settlement. You could also get a refund annuity, guaranteed period annuity, and more. These will be discussed further below.

Private Protection Plan (PPP)

The overall goal of a PPP is to protect your spouse in the event of your death. This is because as long as you stay alive, you're going to get the maximum pension amount and come out with the most monthly pension income. This is what I'll call the 'maximize your pension' strategy. You elect to receive the largest benefit you are eligible to receive. This means you and your spouse must agree to forgo any surviving spouse benefit from the pension, with your spouse agreeing to this plan in writing. Before ever agreeing to this option, your spouse will have the peace of mind knowing that you have already put in place a Private Plan survivor benefit that has more flexibility and may produce more income.

The drawback here is that when you purchase the Private Plan, you usually have to show evidence of good health, which may include a physical examination and underwriting. As noted above, if you have health problems, you may not be able to qualify, and a survivor option from your pension plan may be your only choice. Remember, a big advantage of choosing a survivor option from your pension plan is that you can't be rejected based on your health or anything else. If in doubt, please "go shopping" with a qualified "defensive" planner compare. You have nothing to lose and could gain hundreds of thousands of dollars during retirement, build equity, increase flexibility, and not disinherit your kids or estate.

However, if you are healthy and live a low-risk life, it is worth at least considering a PPP as an alternative to the survivor option from your pension. The PPP may save you hundreds of thousands of dollars and may eliminate one or more of the various disadvantages mentioned in the prior section. How does the PPP work? The basic idea is you purchase a PPP to make up all the lost pension money that your spouse would have received with a spousal survivor option in the event that you die. Remember, you need this if you don't pick a pension survivor option because in the event of your death, your pension *poof* disappears.

To set up the PPP, you don't want to call just any company or agent. You need a very qualified "defensive" professional who can help determine if an alternative program will be able to equal the survivor income your spouse could receive from your pension, had you chosen a 100% or 50% or whatever survivor option that you desire. You also need a qualified company to purchase the plan through. With the right company and expert agent, you can get the necessary guidance and professionalism to set everything up and to settle the claim if the worst happens and you die. Let's turn to some math again.

PPP Advantages

How does this all work? The goal is to provide a monthly income equal to the survivor benefit available from your pension plan in the most economical and flexible manner possible. The flexibility will let you surrender the PPP if your spouse dies before you. Remember, the reason you're doing this PPP is to protect your spouse if you die before he or she does. If your spouse dies before you, then the issue of your spouse outliving you is no longer relevant. If you take a spousal survivor benefit with your pension, you likely have a permanent reduction even if your spouse dies. With a private product, you can just surrender the plan and get money back.

Another advantage is what we call 'cash value.' The cash value is available as it accumulates in your PPP. You can access it. You can withdraw money or use it as collateral for loans. This can be very beneficial in emergencies. However, it is normally not advisable to access your cash value via loans (which accrue interest) because loans will reduce the death benefit intended for the survivor.

You can also specify contingent beneficiaries. If you and your spouse both die, your estate would receive the entire death benefit, unlike a pension that will just disappear. Remember Mandy and Mario. They fly internationally regularly in retirement, and they always have a concern in the back of their minds that something could happen to them either during travel or in-country when touring abroad. A PPP would ensure that, God forbid, they die together in some accident, Mandy's PPP will pass any excess money on to their kids or other contingent beneficiary(ies). Once again, they get peace of mind.

Moreover, this PPP death benefit could be substantial, depending on the size of your plan. These benefits are received Federal Income tax free. Doesn't it make sense to pass it on to the heirs of your estate rather than back to the "black hole" of the pension fund? For state employees, I say, "Pass your money to your <u>estate</u>, rather than <u>the State</u>."

You can also save money compared to your pension reduction. If you purchase a PPP, it can be less outlay than the reduction in the survivor option. With pensions that have cost-of-living increases built into them (COLA pensions), we design level payments in the PPP versus increasing annual cost because of the COLA. See the illustration below using a 2% COLA. This gets a little confusing, and I or someone at my company would be glad to discuss how this arrangement will impact the various components of your policy.

Year	Max Check		Payment		Net Income			Reduced Survivor Option	
1	$3,000.00	-	$500	=	$2,500.00	per month	versus	$2,400.00	per month
6	$3,312.24	-	$500	=	$2,812.24	per month	versus	$2,649.79	per month
11	$3,656.98	-	$500	=	$3,156.98	per month	versus	$2,925.59	per month
21	$4,457.84	-	$500	=	$3,957.84	per month	versus	$3,566.27	per month

The idea is that you choose no surviving spouse pension option but instead take your full $3,000 pension amount. Then you purchase a PPP for less cost than the "spread" (the difference between the single-life income and the survivor benefit). This means in year 1 you would get

$3,000 per month in your pension benefit and pay $500 of that for your payment. You would be left with $2,500 per month for that first year (as opposed to $2,400 per month with a 100% surviving spouse option). In year 6, your pension payment would be around $3,657 per month. Your premium would remain the same $500. This means you would keep $2,812 per month for you to enjoy. If you had taken the reduced 100% survivor option, you would only be receiving $2,650 per month starting in year 6.

If you die in those first five years, your pension will disappear since you didn't elect any survivor benefit for your pension. That sounds terrible, except that you have a balloon tax-free death benefit on yourself at the time of your death. Those proceeds are large enough to provide at least the same benefit as the LOVE OPTION. Be careful here to choose an experienced "defensive" advisor team that has done hundreds or thousands of these plans, or your spouse might not be adequately covered.

Your surviving spouse has many options on how to get the money if you die. He or she can match the monthly benefit of the pension survivor option (for instance, decide to match the $2,650 reduced survivor payout in year 6). The spouse could take a lump sum, income tax-free benefit instead. Then they can invest that lump sum and only draw out the monthly income they need (if any) to live each month. Other options are available depending on the survivor's financial needs, health, etcetera at the time of the settlement.

Let's close out the story of our fictitious couple Mandy and Mario with a final scenario. Let's say she was referred to a qualified "defensive" professional by another friend who retired previously. She and Mario sat down and carefully walked through their options. After fully discussing their life situation and retirement goals, they decided to make the excellent decision to buy a PPP and elect to take no surviving spouse option for her pension. This means Mandy gets her full $3,000 per month pension benefit at retirement. To cover Mario, she purchased a PPP, expecting to live many years.

In this scenario, unfortunately, let's say Mandy had a tragic accident, no fault of her own, and passed away shortly into retirement. Since she didn't elect any survivor benefit, her pension is, sadly, gone. But Mandy was smart to prepare for this scenario by previously purchasing a PPP with $500,000 death benefit. Now, Mario has many options. He can:

1. Take a $500,000 lump sum, income tax-free. This money is available to save or use as needed, but every case is different, so make sure there's enough.

2. Take $2,524 monthly income for life with no beneficiaries (single life annuity).

3. Take $2,376 monthly income for life with a refund of the unused portion of the $500,000, if premature death occurs (refund annuity).

4. Take $2,515 monthly income for life with a guaranteed 10-year period. If death occurs before 10 years, the remaining payments of the 10 years are continued to your named beneficiary (10-year Certain Annuity).

5. Take $2,362 monthly income for life with a guaranteed 20-year period. If death occurs before 20 years, the remaining payments of the 10 years are continued to your named beneficiary (20-year Certain Annuity).

6. Take $1,667 monthly income without depleting the principal sum, assuming 4% earnings on $500,000 (interest-only option). So, the balance would go to his children or estate.

Again, please note that the dollar amounts above are just for illustrative purposes. Actual annuity rates depend on market rates and will fluctuate. The main takeaway is that using a PPP gives your spouse many excellent options when the terrible reality of death takes you. And you don't have to lock in to any one option at the start of retirement, unlike the almost-always permanent "taxable" monthly spousal survivor benefit you must elect before even entering into retirement. In other words, choices don't have to be made until death happens, rather than the day (or months before) you retire.

Doesn't it make sense to give your spouse the flexibility to choose a benefit based on his or her needs down the road? Which one of us can truly know what we'll need even a year from now? It is certainly extremely difficult to know your spouse's financial, physical, and other needs 5, 10, or more years after retirement, once you're gone. You just need to know what PPP is best to replace the surviving spouse pension benefit. This can be tricky, which is why you want to work with a qualified professional.

Sample X-Ray

To aid you in making defined benefit pension decisions, let me introduce what I call a defined benefit pension X-Ray. I use this two-to-three-page tool to examine someone's defined benefit pension and help him or her understand what choices to make. Let's look at a sample X-Ray below.

John and Jane Jenkins are married. John is retiring at age 53. His current salary is $110,000. We'll estimate his yearly salary increases at 3%. His Average Final Compensation will be $120,000, and he will have 30 YOS at retirement. If he took no surviving spouse benefit, he would get his full $6,000. However, he is considering choosing the 100% survivor option, which would reduce his pension to $5,100 per month, which is a reduction of $900. See the chart below:

	Monthly Income	
	Both	Spouse Only
Option 1: Single Life Income	$6,000	$0
Option 2: Reduced Pension with a Survivor Benefit	$5,100	$5,100
Monthly Reduction	($900)	
Maximum Income to Age 80	$2,667,687	
Survivor Option Income to Age 80	$2,267,534	
Total Benefit Loss if Retiree Lives to Age 80	($400,153)	
Percentage Loss of Income	15%	

The Need: John needs to ensure Jane gets monthly income in case he dies before her during retirement. The Common Solution: Take the reduced retirement income to guarantee the Spouse a survivor income. The Problem: Taking the 100% surviving spouse option potentially causes John to lose out on over $400,000 if he ends up living to age 80. See the following chart to see the potential lost pension income.

John and Jane Jenkins: Options					
Retiree Age	Single Life Annuity	Survivor Annuity	Reduced Benefit (Monthly)	Reduced Benefit (Annual)	Reduced Benefit (Cumulative)
53	$6,000	$5,100	($900)	($10,800)	($10,800)
65	$7,609	$6,468	($1,141)	($13,697)	($158,548)
70	$8,401	$7,141	($1,260)	($15,123)	($231,253)
75	$9,276	$7,884	($1,391)	($16,697)	($311,526)
80	$10,241	$8,705	($1,536)	($18,434)	**($400,153)**
Total	$2,667,687	$2,267,534			

Notice that the "cost" (sometimes called the "spread" or "delta") gets larger each year. This is because picking that survivor option means you also pick a COLA (cost of living adjustment) on a smaller pension. Mathematically, the Cost increases each year and in 27 years the cost is over $1,500 vs $900!

Out to life expectancy, this is a $400,000 problem for life, not a $900 per month problem.

You are giving up a lot of money by taking the 100% survivor option. Granted, it's easy: just check the box and be done. Also, it is available to all retirees; there are no qualification requirements. But then there are the downsides we've already discussed. To review:

1. Reduction benefit - see above. (note, this is only to age 80, the cost increases if he lives longer)

2. No flexibility. If Jane (the spouse) predeceases John (the pensioner), there is no refund. But possibly increased annuity for John (if the pension has a "pop-up" provision).

3. No cash value (equity) that is accessible during John's lifetime.

4. No benefits for the children. Nothing passes to the children after John and Jane die.

5. COLA is smaller on the reduced annuity vs. the single life annuity.

6. Jane (the spouse) cannot opt for a lump-sum, income-tax free benefit, or other settlement options...just a taxable monthly income.

Given these various disadvantages and the potentially large, accumulated reduction in pension income, John and Jane Jenkins should strongly consider taking the single life option from John's pension and providing Jane a spousal survivor benefit using a PPP instead.

The goals for a PPP would be:

1. Take John's maximum retirement annuity: $6,000 per month.

2. Provide a minimum additional survivor benefit of $5,100 per month for Jane.

3. Gain the maximum flexibility with the PPP.

4. Accomplish John and Jane's objectives and possibly leave a benefit to their children.

We will send you free X-Rays like this if you provide us with a benefit estimate from your pension. This benefit estimate is like a snapshot in time, and we will construct future projections using projected COLAs out to life expectancies. This projection is like a motion picture to help you see your pension through the years. Email your pension estimate to Info@RetirementNationwide.com. We will have a qualified "defensive" planner contact you for some additional information and get you an X-Ray.

Summary of Private Plans

The goal of PPP is to make it more likely that you will come out ahead with more retirement money and more flexibility than if you simply 'check the box' to take a reduced pension payment to cover your surviving spouse. You want to "maximize your pension income" and still provide a survivor payout for your spouse at least equal to what a reduced survivor option would provide per month. A PPP lets you do this with more flexibility (plus equity) than your pension plan survivor choices. The equity can also become a residual estate passed to your children, preferred charities, or heirs.

In addition, a PPP gives you quite a few extra benefits. You may end up with more overall retirement money. You have flexibility. If your spouse dies first, you can simply surrender the policy, receive any cash value, and continue receiving your maximum pension benefits. Or you could choose to keep the plan for your estate and let them take over the payments for it if they have the available monthly income (I personally plan to do this, if needed).

As noted, your PPP builds cash value, some of which can be accessed during your lifetime tax-free. Your PPP also passes to your estate rather than just stopping like your pension. This benefit also passes to your estate income tax-free.

Your spouse also has a great deal of flexible options when you die. At a minimum, your spouse can receive the same survivor benefit as what he or she would have received from the reduced survivor option. In addition, your spouse has other options like taking a lump-sum tax-free. Very importantly, the choice doesn't need to be made after your death.

There are challenges with PPP. You have to qualify, and companies discriminate if you aren't in good health. Plus, the payment you must pay will be larger if you're older. Thus, the age of the client at the time of purchasing is critical. Start early and have that guarantee locked in at a younger age before you develop a health problem that could disqualify you from getting a PPP. This is also a "unilateral contract" the company can NEVER drop your coverage if you make the required payments.

Make sure auto-payments are set up, and always be disciplined to use the extra pension income to cover your payment every month.

Despite the challenges, PPPs have so many advantages. One of the best rewards is the peace of mind knowing that you have optimally provided for both you and your spouse, regardless of who dies first. You don't have to just gamble with a reduced pension benefit in hopes that your spouse doesn't die first. You can be confident that you've planned well for your family, which is a feeling worth much more than money.

Additional Questions about Private Plans

By now, I hope you agree that the Private Plan option is at least worth looking into. Perhaps you see the wisdom in taking the maximum pension amount and providing your spouse with an alternative Private Plan policy. Many questions likely come to your mind. Let's ask and answer some.

How can I know if I qualify? You can't know until you apply and are accepted for the PPP. The company will decide and either make you an offer or decline you. There is no cost or obligation to find out if you qualify through a qualified financial professional.

Can't I do better with my money than buying a PPP? You might be able to do better than the growth of the plan's cash value, but most important is the death benefit. It is a balloon payment and can be many times greater than the payments that you've made. Also, proceeds are income tax-free to your beneficiary. It provides the guarantees of payment that you need to provide for your spouse. Unless you're fabulously wealthy, it is unlikely that you can purchase enough assets before your death to produce a reliable, monthly income for your surviving spouse. Plus, the risk is all yours when going with traditional investments. A well-constructed PPP gives you a guarantee of payment upon your death. Your spouse can then use the lump-sum proceeds to purchase an annuity equivalent to the survivor benefit he or she would have gotten from your pension.

Should I wait until retirement to start the PPP? You could wait, but the longer you wait the riskier it gets to qualify. Your health may change while you wait the final few years until retirement. The sooner you put the policy in force, the better. Also, the younger you are, the lower the payments will be. However, make sure you have a PPP in force before you opt out of the guaranteed survivor option from your pension.

Should I really get this PPP before retirement? Won't that mean I'll have to pay for it before I get my pension money? Yes, it is true that setting up your PPP before retirement means you'll have to make your payments before you retire. But yes, you really should get your PPP early, if you can. This is probably the most frequently asked question, so let me give you five reasons to start early.

1. **You are most likely healthier now than you will be as you age.** Right now, you can hopefully get the most favorable rates you will ever be able to get. If you are like most people over age 50, your health will get worse rather than better year by year. By starting early, you can lock into earlier rates, which are certainly lower than the rates in the years to come.

2. **You are younger now than you will be tomorrow.** Did you know that you'll never be as young again as you are right now? That's obvious, but even if you are just as healthy five years from now as you are today, rates always go up based on your age. We're taught not to discriminate in life, but these companies always look more favorably on those who are younger. This is because older age means a higher risk of death, on average. So, start sooner rather than later. A good advisor can quantify the differences in costs and give you choices that fit your unique situation.

3. **It's easier to pay now than after retirement.** It is likely that today you are taking home more income than you will bring home after you retire. It may not feel like it, but it should be easier to make payments using your larger pre-retirement dollars rather than waiting until a pay decrease in retirement. Get into the habit of making your payment now, so that you're used to it once retirement comes along. We have many clients who make these contributions in lieu of their 457, 403b, 401k (above the match) contributions for better tax diversification of their retirement.

4. **You get the death benefit as soon as the policy is in effect.** If you start the policy early, you are covered in case of your death. Thus, if you die before retirement, your spouse will receive both the policy death benefit and a survivor benefit from your pension.

5. **Consider peace of mind.** Probably one of the most important aspects of pension option planning is to start as soon as you can so you don't have a big mess to sort out late in your life.[38] What a relief it is to retire, knowing that you will receive the maximum monthly pension payment and have a robust Private Protection Plan already in force to provide for your spouse if you die.

Have I persuaded you to consider the 'maximize your pension' strategy by using a PPP? For those healthy, married retirees with pensions, I truly believe in the 'maximize your pension' strategy that utilizes a PPP. By this I mean you elect to receive the maximum monthly benefit and take no spousal survivor benefit. I know it is very difficult to go 'against the grain' and forego the safety of that spousal benefit, but that is where the PPP comes in. With a proper plan in place, you get the best of both worlds: a maximum pension and the guarantee that your spouse will be taken care of when the inevitable event of death takes you.

What to do When You Don't Qualify

What if you consider this Private Plan idea, apply for it through a qualified adviser, and get rejected? Maybe you already have tried to get protection before but have some specific illness that makes you unqualified. What do you do then? Well, then your best option is to go with a spousal survivor benefit. Let me explain more about the survivor benefit.

Understand that when you pick to have a spousal survivor benefit, you are, in effect, buying a life insurance policy from your pension. The premium is the amount your pension is reduced by. For instance, if you received $3,000 with no survivor benefit, you now will get $2,400

---

[38] Strongly consider reading my year 2020 book, Die Neatly. It covers many more very beneficial topics.

with a 100% spousal option. This $600 difference can be thought of as your pension-enforced life insurance premium that is taken out of your monthly benefit. The pension plan then pockets this $600 month after month, knowing it may have to eventually pay out a benefit to your spouse upon your death. Thus, even if you can't qualify for a superior PPP, taking a spousal survivor benefit is, in effect, buying a guaranteed life insurance policy from your pension.[39]

How good is the pension's life insurance product? Let me present some facts, and then you can decide how attractive this option is to you.

1. You pay premiums your entire life, which increase at 2-3% per year.

2. You pay the same high premium as a 65-year-old smoker with emphysema.

3. There's no cash value or equity while you're alive.

4. There's also no lump sum tax-free benefit or accelerated benefit for terminal illness (or long-term care).

5. Your spouse is the only beneficiary (nothing goes to your children or estate).

6. The death benefit is a taxable monthly income for your spouse only (no other options).

7. If your spouse dies first, you still pay the premiums, but no one will ever get the survivor benefit (assuming your pension has no 'pop-up' clause). Even with a pop-up pension, the premiums stop, but you get nothing back.

Does this sound like a good policy to purchase? This is what you are 'buying' when you 'check the box' to elect a survivor benefit for your spouse. We know that over 75% of married retirees with defined benefit pensions take the LOVE OPTION, even though they are terrible

---

[39] Some of this section has been adapted from Chapter 8 of my 2020 book, Die Neatly.

purchases when you consider all of the negatives above. This is why I call the reduced spousal option the "worst life insurance policy ever (unless you can't qualify for a better one because of your health)."

So, why do people buy that policy? Some people don't qualify, but the biggest reason people take the spousal option is because they simply don't know they have an alternative solution. Another reason is because of bad advice. My biggest problem is when healthy married retirees take a reduced pension without even shopping around for a better solution. Sometimes it's their financial planner who is not experienced in Defensive Financial Planning and doesn't realize that taking the surviving spouse reduced pension option is, in effect, buying a terrible life insurance policy with many problems (listed prior).

Sometimes an employee can have so much trust in the pension that they don't want to take the seeming risk of going with a PPP. However, these mutual companies have been in business for over 140 years with high financial ratings (and will no doubt continue doing business long after all of us are gone). I love to tell my Washington retirees that these companies were doing business before Washington become a state in 1889!

Then there's the few who look into a PPP but can't qualify. This gets us back to what to do if you can't get a PPP because of medical reasons. The big ones are recent cancers, heart conditions, or diabetes. If you try but are denied for a PPP, you are basically forced into 'buying' this worst life insurance policy ever. At least you know you tried to get a better plan rather than just taking the survivor benefit by default.

Chapter Conclusion

Planning for retirement takes time," people don't plan to fail, they fail to plan". If you are blessed with a pension, understanding your pension benefit should be a high priority for you in the present. You don't want any surprises when you retire. It should be a time of celebration and rewards, rather than a string of unwelcome news. If you're getting close to retirement, have a defined benefit pension, and are relatively healthy, you can still "maximize your pension" by purchasing the RIGHT PPP from a qualified "defensive" advisor or team.

As we saw with Mandy and Mario throughout this chapter, nobody can know what path the future will take us on. Maybe we will live many years and accomplish all our retirement goals. Or tragedy might happen, including premature death or serious illness. While we can't control many things, we can plan wisely to help positively shape whatever may be ahead for us. That is the goal of Pension Option Planning: to help you live better no matter what life throws your way.

Whether you are excited about the PPP I've presented in this chapter or not, it would be wise of you to continue learning more about this approach. This spousal benefit protection is what we, at Retirement Nationwide, Inc., specialize in. I have a passion to help as many people as possible with what I consider to be the biggest retirement decision my clients with defines benefit pensions will ever make. If done wrong, it costs hundreds of thousands of dollars, gives up equity, and doesn't transfer to your children. If you have a pension, don't procrastinate with this plan (get professional financial help now!). If you have an offensive planner (most financial planners) who also doesn't agree with this, please GET A SECOND OPINION. We work jointly with many financial planners to do what's best for you.

Here is one final, true story. At the time of this writing, I heard about a police detective who was retiring. I called him, and he was very skeptical when I first explained who I was and what I was offering. Thankfully, he met with me, and I showed him the big problems with taking the reduced pension option. After seeing the facts, he bought about a PPP for $800 per month. He's happy, and I helped another great retiree. I thanked him for his service and saved him Hundreds of Thousands of dollars (if he lives to his life expectancy). It was fortunate that his friend and many like him thought enough of both me and them to introduce us.

This needs to be the norm. Through education (such as the information in this book), we can get there and help so many more. I say, "Friends don't let healthy married retiree friends take reduced pensions without shopping!" I'd love to personally help you, and I believe that no firm specializes in this "pension option planning" more than Retirement Nationwide, Inc. Still, there are other good agents familiar with this concept. If your advisor would like to work with us, we'd love to help him or her help you. Just let us know that you have another advisor who is open-minded about math. We will work together and shop all trusted companies (not just companies some advisors are "loyal" to) to do what's best for you.

There are also many good companies to consider. It is up to you to decide how you are going to get the service and products you deserve. Make sure the company you contract with has solid performance records rather than just promises. Use ratings agencies to compare companies.[40] Mutual companies give you part ownership, so consider ones which have been going strong for at least 140-150 years. Look at how the companies have managed through difficult economic times, and work with a firm who can represent many companies and get the best PPP for you.

I also believe that pension-related decisions are too complicated for most retirees to plan and decide on their own. Expert advice from a qualified "defensive" advisor is essential. Once again, we, at Retirement Nationwide, Inc., are ready to assist, so give us a chance to serve you!

Addendum: Widows and Orphans

I'm age 69 at the time of writing this in 2024. I have over 40 years of experience and have served thousands of clients and worked with hundreds of advisors. It would be a comfortable retirement for me if I just "stopped working," but my work has never been just about earning a living for me. When I help someone start a PPP, I promise to serve them for as long as I am able. So, to stop working would be to stop serving, in my view. And I have made commitments to so many people to pay death claims and look after widows and orphans (see the Bible verse, James 1:27).

I plan to follow a great mentor and friend, Ed VanVliet (a retired advisor with my first company). I saw him at a restaurant parking lot when he

---

[40] Use ratings agencies like A.M. Best, Moody's, Standard & Poor's, and Fitch.

was age 80. After some "chit-chat," I asked him why he's still working. His response (paraphrased):

"After 60 years in the business, I made a lot of promises to beneficiaries. I only work 8-10 hours per week, but last month I paid 12 death claims, including to the widow of my best friend. You can delegate a lot of things, but that is a commitment that I want to continue doing myself for as long as I can."

How impressive! I want to publicly commit to the same as Ed. I commit to my friends and clients that if I'm coherent and can move and talk, I will be there (with a lot younger successor advisors on my team) to pay the claims that so many have diligently paid into for years. To the best of my knowledge, I remember every claim I've ever paid (and the impact for that family). At funerals, wakes, or memorial services, I ask myself how many other people will be delivering this widow or widower hundreds of thousands or millions of dollars rather than just hugs, flowers, or a nice card. We, in this business, make a difference when people need it the most.

As Defensive Retirement Specialists, we really do help others and keep families in their homes and living good lifestyles. We keep businesses afloat and pay those ugly estate taxes for "pennies on the dollar." Reach out if you need help. I'm still accepting clients.

Advisors who are open to coaching in serving these great clients please join the movement by joining the Advisor's Lounge via www.retirementnationwide.com. Too many retirees aren't getting served and they need our help.

Part 4

Other Living

Money Machines

Introducing Other Living Money Machines

In Part 1 through Part 3, we dealt with Human Life Value, social security, and defined benefit pensions. Many of you are beyond your working years, so you probably won't grow your earned income much unless you invent something, start a new business, or win the lottery. Maybe you're already drawing social security, and you might not have a defined benefit pension. Do you have enough resources to enjoy retirement? We already said in Part 2-C that the number one fear of retirees in America is "outliving their money."

Even people with over $1,000,000 in an IRA or similar account like a 401(k), may not have enough money when considering market fluctuations, inflation, and lifestyle choices. To determine how much money you need, we once again use the 4% rule we first spoke of in Part 1-C. To review, the 4% rule says you can generally safely take out 4% of an asset each year without reducing the principal if it is managed properly. A simple example can be seen with the $1,000,000 in an IRA mentioned above. If this IRA is properly invested in safe and reliable investments, a 4% annual return would be $40,000 per year. This means you could take out that $40,000 per year and never drop below the initial $1,000,000. Ideally, you could take out a monthly amount of $3,333. This strategy means that you probably won't deplete your principal, and you won't run out of money during your lifetime.

The problem is that even if you are very blessed to have a $1,000,000 investment balance at retirement in stocks, mutual funds, or various retirement accounts, that 4% is only $40,000 per year, but it is also not guaranteed. It may sound okay in the year 2024, but inflation will continue to degrade the spending power of this $40,000. Plus, some people tend to follow the market too closely and take out too much money when the market is up. They don't plan for the market corrections (big drops) that always happen eventually.

There are risks of any "withdrawal" plan, and some people are living longer and longer. This means the fear of running out of money is very real. This chapter is meant to introduce supplemental strategies to fight back that fear through spinning up other living money machines. We've already hinted at various financial tools that guarantee income for your lifetime, like the tried-and-true annuity family of products. There are several products, but I'm going to limit the discussion to the two most popular guaranteed income vehicles. These are Guaranteed Lifetime Income Annuities and Charitable Remainder Trusts, also known as GLIAs and CRTs respectively.

Guaranteed Lifetime Income Annuities (GLIAs)

A guaranteed lifetime income annuity is a contract usually issued by a life insurance company. You pay a lump sum of money to the company, and the company pays a monthly or annual guaranteed payment for the rest of your life.

If you're healthy and believe that you will live a long time, this could be a good deal. However, if you die early, the company "wins" and keeps your money. There are many payment methods where you can assure that the principal payment (or more) be paid to your estate if you die early. [Please see Part 3-B for several pay-out options.]

I could elaborate and go deeper on this very important product, but I'm not worthy to even summarize what the great Tom Hegna wrote in his book, "Paychecks and Playchecks." He makes it clear why every retirement portfolio should have some percentage invested in immediate (or deferred) income annuities to guarantee at least some stream of income for life. Please read his book!

The part of GLIAs that I like the most are the "mortality credits" (also explored in Tom's book). Basically, the older you are when you buy the GLIA, the bigger the "payout" rates. The payout rate is based on interest rates and life expectancy. Here's a simple table based on annuity rates from a major life insurance company. This isn't a guarantee of future results but notice the amazing payout rates between ages 70 to 80.

GLIA Payout Rates for $100,000 Investment*					
Age	Monthly Income	Annual Income	Payout Rate**	Breakeven Year***	15-Year Payout
65	$570	$6,840	6.84%	14.6	$102,600
70	$657	$7,894	7.88%	12.7	$118,620
75	$779	$9,348	9.35%	10.7	$140,220
80	$951	$11,412	11.41%	8.8	$171,180
86	$1,192	$14,304	14.30%	7	$214,560

*These are hypothetical rates. For actual rates, please get quotes from at least three highly-rated life insurance companies from a broker who specializes in annuities. We highly recommend some form of refund annuity or life with period certain to protect against early death of the annuitant.

**These are payout rates, not a rate of return. The annuity is paying out principal and interest.

***The year that all of your original investment money is paid back to you.

As you can see, the payouts for ages 75 to 86 represent payout rates guaranteed for life that are higher than many analysts would project stock market returns. Please note you are dispersing principal and interest, so when you die it stops (without other payout options that would be less than illustrated).

Again, the companies know through actuarial science that "life expectancy" is a predictable risk. This is why they can sell annuities. They know that the shorter an annuitant is expected to live, the more money that they can pay out. This is the opposite of life insurance where the life insurance company wants you to live a very long time. With annuities such as GLIAs, the companies know that, on average, people who die sooner pay for the "long-livers". A good "defensive retirement specialist" can find the best annuities and other products to fit your needs.

Charitable Remainder Trusts (CRTs)

Many people are very charitable and want to leave money after their death to charities. Others have concerns about "living too long" so are conservative about how much they give to others while still living. They want to make sure their lifestyle (and their family's lifestyle) isn't compromised. Still others want to take advantage of tax laws (both income and estate taxes) and want to minimize taxes as they maximize and even leverage their charitable gift giving.

If you have wealth and want to leave money to charity but also create an income stream for your life (and the life of your spouse, if married) and desire huge tax breaks, consider establishing a CRT.

With a CRT, you donate assets (Real Estate, investment portfolios, etc.) to the CRT. The CRT then holds ownership until your death (or the later death of you and your spouse). Then the trust transfers the ownership to your charity (a church, nonprofit organization, foundation, etc.). In the meantime, the trust pays out income back to you. The payout is usually about 5% for life (or the life of the last to die of two spouses). This is a great lifetime income (money machine) for life with many advantages, such as:

1. You get a substantial income and tax deduction for giving away assets to a charity. Note that the IRS makes you discount the deduction because it's not a "present interest gift" (Google that term), but it is still a large percentage of the value depending on your age and lifespan. You get to take this deduction every year until the discounted value is exhausted. Had you sold an asset and then given the proceeds to charity, you would have paid up to 21% (2024 rate) in Federal capital gains taxes and possibly also paid State capital gains taxes depending on where you live. With the CRT, the value of the property is excluded from income and estate taxes.

2. The charity is blessed to receive a large donation that they will inherit upon your death (or your spouse's death).

3. The income from the trust is taxable as per Federal or State income tax, but it is for your LIFE; this is another Money Machine for Life

4. The CRT provides a win/win situation, except in the case that your heirs want to inherit the property. They may understand, but there are ways to replace that value if desired. Read on for some suggestions.

Maximizing GLIAs and CRTs

GLIAs work best for healthy people who are between 75 and 85. At 75 today, if you are a healthy, non-tobacco user, you have a good chance of living 20 more years. With people living longer, one of the fastest growing segments of our population are Centenarians (people over 100 years old).[41] By moving some assets into a GLIA (not even a large percentage), this income, like Social Security retirement or a defined benefit pension, is guaranteed for life by the financial stability of the life insurance company. I recommend mutual companies with high ratings founded in the mid or late 1800s. These companies were bailing out banks in the Great Depression and were very stable through both World Wars.

This GLIA is also excluded from your estate if your estate if you take the highest payout (Life only). For example, $1,000,000 at age 75 might have a 9.5% payout rate. This means $95,000 per year for life. After 20 years, you would receive $1,900,000 in income. If this money isn't qualified (not in an IRA, 401(k), etc.), then over 90% of it is tax-free until the $1,000,000 is paid back to you.

On the downside, if you died just after year one ended, you would have received $95,000 but lose the 'balance' of $905,000. This can be a huge risk unless protected, at least that money is excluded from your estate and not subject to estate tax liability.

---

[41] More people are living to be 100: Here's why. Feb. 07, 2023. https://thehill.com/changing-america/well-being/longevity/3847532-more-people-are-living-to-be-100-heres-why/

Most annuitants take some form of 'period-certain' or refund annuity to mitigate the risk of dying in the first few years. You will take less than $95,000 as you will be paying an "insurance premium" that effectively reduces your payout to guarantee a payout period or amount. Most of the balance is included in your estate now also. You can purchase a "refund annuity" or a long enough "period certain" to guaranteed that all of the principal is paid out.

Wealth Replacement Trusts (WRTs)

Another idea to consider is a Wealth Replacement Trust (WRT). This is a way to replace the initial investment into an annuity with a trust funded by life insurance. With our $1,000,000 GLIA example, you would use a WRT funded by a $1,000,000 life insurance policy. This works best for healthy people around age 70. Once you hit your late 70s, the life insurance premium is probably too high, and you might not be insurable enough to get a good rating. In your early 60s the annuity payout rate is not high enough to justify the investment. Find a good life insurance and annuity expert to see if this strategy may work for you.

Ideally, a WRT will be an Irrevocable Life Insurance Trust (ILIT), so the $1,000,000 is not included in the estate for estate tax exposure. The best policies for married couples are called "survivorship" or "second to die" policies. This means that right after the second death, even over age 100, the policy death benefit is paid to the trust and excluded from Federal Estate Taxation.

For years, I've shared this concept, and it works best when both spouses are healthy, conservative, and really dislike estate taxes. This WRT is also recommended when you set up your CRT because, for example, say you just gave away a large parcel of property (like a commercial Real Estate building) to the future of a charity. Your kids might be appalled because they thought they were going to inherit the property. Do they really want the building? Maybe they do, but maybe they just want the value it represents. So, if they received the building, it's possible 40-50% would be subject to estate taxes.

With the WRT, like with the GLIA, upon the second death the life insurance proceeds are paid out income and estate tax-free if you set it up right. Then you can leave as much as you want to your kids, grandkids, and beyond. Seek professional help from a qualified estate planning attorney.

Chapter Conclusion

If your goal is to create an income that you can't outlive no matter what, you should find a great adviser to help navigate these advanced strategies and GLIA, CRT, WRT, and ILIT acronyms. Come up with a strategy that uses some of your assets to go into a CRT and/or a GLIA, especially if you're healthy enough to qualify for a life insurance policy funding a WRT. If you are married, consider the income for both lives and the life insurance death benefit will be paid right after the second death to replace or partially replace the asset that was either given away to charity or invested in a GLIA to 'convert' the asset to income. Confusing? Really can be.

That's why financial professionals exist to help you navigate these incredible financial opportunities to minimize their income and estate taxes and maximize the transfer of their assets to their heirs and charities.

Book Summary

Money Machines for life are your most valuable assets. Whether Human Life Value (HLV), Social Security Retirement, Defined Benefit Pensions, GLIAs, or CRTs, the income from these depends on you being alive. With human life value, the more educated, talented, and driven you are, the greater income you can generate. It is the foundation that makes you able to spin up all the other money machines over your life, such as qualifying for and maximizing Social Security Retirement or working hard for a company or government agency that offers a defined benefit pension. Then you can build up great wealth to fund GLIAs and CRTs once you get toward the end of your life.

Some of you are fortunate enough to have the trifecta by your 50s or 60s: decades of high HLV income, maximized Social Security Benefits, and a large defined benefit pension. Please enjoy your hard work and good fortune. No matter where you are at, don't take your situation for granted. If you're just starting out or struggling to build wealth in your midlife years, don't fall into the trap of alluring 'Wall Street' investments. Too many people spend countless hours studying their investment portfolios and very little time studying how to maximize their Money Machines for Life.

This book has been about returning to the basics, and those basics begin with you. That is why Part 1 was all about you and your Human Life Value. Understand your worth, grow your skills through education and training, and think beyond your current capabilities. See your value as a person, to yourself, your family, and the world. Every one of us is given an 'irreplaceable' money machine that is our ability to work and earn a living. Unfortunately, money machines can break down and run out, sometimes much too soon. This is why you want to take wise steps to protect yourself through various financial products.

Part 2 explained how to boost your social security retirement benefits and when to draw those benefits. Begin playing the 'wage base' game at a young age. Track your progress yearly to see how close to the maximum wage base you can reach. Do the math yourself on when to draw your benefits. We saw that **the best time to draw your Social Security retirement benefit is as soon as you can UNLESS you will get hit with a penalty for working too much.**

Part 3 focused on learning about and maximizing your pension, including protecting your spouse without having to take a reduced pension benefit at retirement. Carefully look at your defined benefit pension (if you don't have one, you need to save even more to make up lost income at retirement). If you are blessed with a defined benefit pension and are married, consider your spousal benefit choice carefully. One of the biggest financial decisions you'll ever make is finding the best way to provide a survivor benefit for your spouse. PLEASE DO NOT AUTOMATICALLY take a reduced pension (if you're healthy) without shopping and comparing private financial products that are likely better options. Find the beauty and value of a PPP for your spouse, rather than relying on your rigid institutional pension with no choices or flexibility. Do it early while you're young and healthy and save potentially hundreds of thousands of dollars, create tax free equity, have flexibility, and if desired leave an estate for your children. Get that PEACE OF MIND.

The final Part 4 can be thought of as the cherry on top of a well-lived life, allowing you to further bless and protect yourself and those you care about. Consider Guaranteed Lifetime Income Annuities (GLIAs) and Charitable Remainder Trusts (CRTs) once you've gotten all your other money machines for life in order and running well.

Plan Today!

Let me once again quote one of my mentors: **"It's amazing that people spend a month to plan a week's vacation in Hawaii, and yet they'll work for 30 years but won't take an hour or two to plan the rest of their life."** [42] So true. Please plan. "People don't plan to fail; they just fail to plan."

By reading this book, you have already broken away from most people, and you are proving you want to take steps to secure your financial future that most people don't even realize can be taken. Whether young or old, never stop studying. Don't wait until tomorrow to learn something that can help you live better today. With discipline, sacrifice, and vision, this can be the most rewarding planning you'll ever do.

In fact, many of my clients are over age 60 when they begin studying Social Security and Pension Option Planning (POP). The majority say, "I wish I would have understood and started this Defensive Planning sooner." The younger you are, the more money can compound in your favor. Plus, there is a great chance of minimizing future taxes if you start early.

Beware of termites! Recall that many advisers are "termites" who only recommend term life insurance no matter what. Don't indulge close-minded financial thinking that says you must fit into a certain investment mold regardless of your situation. In 40-plus years, I've found that term insurance has a fantastic place when you are in your early years. You can get millions of dollars of coverage for cheap that protects your family from the loss of your HLV if you die young. We actually broker more term policies and higher death benefits with term insurance than permanent. But, for permanent problems, you need permanent solutions. There's a place for both.

You hopefully will 'outlive' your term life insurance and want to receive the benefits of more costly permanent life insurance as your age and income go up (hopefully your income goes up faster than your age!). Don't ignore the many uses for permanent life insurance, as outlined in

---

[42] Virginia Faust, past director of the Washington State Teacher's Retirement System.

this book. If you have a financial advisor who won't listen to other ideas, just let them "stay in their lane" and manage your investment portfolio (Offensive planning) while you get help from those of us who are trained for Defensive planning.

It's ok to have more than one adviser. In fact, it's a rare expert who can be brilliant on both investments and conservative financial products. Avoid anyone who insists on 'doing it all' for you, sort of like a cult mentality of total commitment to one person or group. This "one stop shopping" can be like asking your oncologist to be your cardiologist. Wise professionals won't be offended when you work with other qualified professionals. They will hopefully be glad for an opportunity to even learn new things from other professionals. This synergistic approach brings clints the best results for the clients.

Much like how many wealthy people recognize the need to have both an accountant and lawyer, get a good offensive and defensive financial expert. I personally recognize that 90% of my peers in the Financial Planning Association (FPA) are better than me at portfolio analysis, asset reallocation, and so on. That isn't my focus, so I listen to the expertise of others.

Likewise, many financial planners rely on our firm and a couple of firms like ours to help their clients with what we've talked about in this book: life insurance, disability insurance, long-term care, PPP, and more. I love to work together for the client's best interest and educate other Certified Financial Planners (CFPs) about the miracle of life insurance. As a resource, I also recommend my first book, "Die Neatly," to learn about Life Insurance 101, disability insurance, and long-term care.

Get Professional Help

I've found few planners over my 40+ years in this great who integrate these Defensive Financial Planning strategies. Most focus instead on how much money they can control for their clients. The focus can too often be on the advisor, only focusing on increasing their AUM (Assets Under Management) and not look at your Defensive Planning also. I recommend you find professionals who will truly listen to you and manage your products best. This means encouraging you in both Offensive and Defensive financial planning. This may take two separate, highly talented advisors. I know I can't be "everything to everybody" and I doubt anyone can.

You owe it to yourself to hire experts who serve your needs. Interview two or three professionals and have all the advisors share information (like doctors) for your overall financial fitness. When someone tells me that they already have an adviser, I ask them what firm their advisor is with. About 95% of the time, it's a firm who specializes in offense and dabbles (even though they say they can do it all) in life insurance, disability, and long-term care. I show them my resume and tell them: "I don't want to undo or compete with the good work your advisor has done. I just want to help you with the "defensive" side (risk management). Like American Football, you be the "head coach" and consider me (and my firm) to be your "defensive coordinators."

At Retirement Nationwide, Inc, we specialize in Defense and defense wins championships. Our advisors are trained in Defensive Retirement Planning that leads to holistic planning. We want to be a resource for protecting and maximizing your living money machines.

As you search for your Defensive Planner, I recommend going outside the firm that your current Financial Planner is with. This way you can better trust second opinions and avoid some conflicts of interest. Many firms like ours will evaluate your life insurance, disability, or long-term care policies to make sure you have options to consider other than just term insurance when appropriate. Money machines are precious and limited things. Please protect them properly as they are gifts from God.

Speaking of faith and higher power, consider a percentage of your money machine income to go to good causes while you live (such as a 10% tithe to church or charity).

Final Thoughts

I hope this book has been enlightening and challenges your paradigm of lifetime income streams of your human life value, social security retirement, defined benefit pensions, and more. If you like it, please order Die Neatly, my first book. Some of that information is included in this book, but there's more on Estate Planning, Legacy Planning, etc. Order both books through www.dieneatly.com. Advisors order in bulk through Retirement Nationwide and join the Advisor's Lounge movement today: www.advisorslounge.com.

God bless you in your financial life and otherwise. Please send me your thoughts, feedback, and questions (jim@retirementnationwide.com). Jim Lusk, CFP, CLU, ChFC, CLF, MEd

Please see the additional resources below:

Websites:

> www.retirementnationwide.com
>
> www.tomhegna.com
>
> www.davidmcknight.com
>
> www.lifehappens.org

Recommended Books:

> Power of Zero, David McKnight
>
> Paychecks & Play Checks, Tom Hegna
>
> Die Neatly, Jim Lusk, CFP, CLU, ChFC
>
> Killing Sacred Cows, Garrett Gunderson
>
> Look Before You LIRP, David McKnight

Acknowledgements, Master Clients and Board of Directors

> Larry Myers (wife Molly)...Brother, Successful Hardware Store Owners
>
> Jaimie Lusk ...daughter, clinical psychologist
>
> Jodi Lusk (husband Tom)...daughter, son-in-law, Parents of my awesome grandkids
>
> Alisha Myers (husband Peter)...Attorney and Deputy Sheriff
>
> Hailey Myers (husband Angel)....Social workers and lineman
>
> Harry Amend (wife Sandy)....retired School Superintendent and teacher
>
> Kevin Cooke (wife Bobbi)...retired County Engineer and teacher
>
> Shon Hocker (wife Carla)...School Superintendent and homemaker
>
> Brian Burnett (wife April) ...Retired Sheriff and church worker
>
> Brian Talbott (wife Trish)....School Superintendent and teacher

Rick Johnson (wife Christina)…Police Chief and Teacher

Kyle Rydell (wife Laura)….Scholl Superintendent and homemaker

Bill Deruyter (wife Anne)…Fire chief and Office manager

Brett Myers (wife Darcell)…Sheriff and Realtor

Jeff Crandell (wife Julie) Estate Planning Attorney and Homemaker

Ryan Crandell (wife Jennifer) Estate Planning Attorney and Homemaker

Made in United States
Troutdale, OR
04/08/2024

19039278R00096